KT-468-975

About this book

KEY TO SYMBOLS

✚	map reference on the fold-out map accompanying this book (see below)	🚌	nearest bus route
✉	address	⛴	nearest riverboat or ferry stop
☎	telephone number	♿	facilities for visitors with disabilities
🕐	opening times	✋	admission charge
🍴	restaurant or café on premises or near by	↔	other nearby places of interest
Ⓜ	nearest métro (underground) train station	❓	tours, lectures or special events
🚆	nearest overground train station	►	indicates the page where you will find a fuller description
		ℹ	tourist infomation

CityPack Paris is divided into six sections to cover the six most important aspects of your visit to Paris. It includes:

- The author's view of the city and its people
- Itineraries, walks and excursions
- The top 25 sights to visit – as selected by the author
- Features about different aspects of the city that make it special
- Detailed listings of restaurants, hotels, shops and nightlife
- Practical information

In addition, easy-to-read side panels provide fascinating extra facts and snippets, highlights of places to visit and invaluable practical advice.

CROSS-REFERENCES

To help you make the most of your visit, cross-references, indicated by ► , show you where to find additional information about a place or subject.

MAPS

- **The fold-out map** in the wallet at the back of the book is a comprehensive street plan of Paris. All the map references given in the book refer to this map. For example, the Musée du Louvre at 99 rue de Rivoli has the following information: ✚ 65, indicating the grid square of the map in which the Musée du Louvre will be found.

- **The city-centre maps** found on the inside front and back covers of the book itself are for quick reference. They show the Top 25 Sights, described on pages 24–48, which are clearly plotted by number (❶ – ㉕, not page number) from west to east across the city.

PRICES

Where appropriate, an indication of the cost of an establishment is given by **£** signs: **£££** denotes higher prices, **££** denotes average prices, while **£** denotes lower charges.

PARIS *life*

A PERSONAL VIEW

The French state

An unmistakable characteristic of France and consequently Paris is the state's top-heavy role. What other industrialised country allows a state bank (Crédit Lyonnais) to run up losses approaching FF60 billion (US$11 billion) in five years? And what other nation offers amnesty to all traffic-offenders when a new president is elected?

Paris remains the powerhouse of the nation, despite repeated government manoeuvres for decentralisation. This is where French socio-cultural trends are born, political battles are fielded and national pride is polished. And yet it remains compact, still bordered by the *portes* (gateways) which keep the less prestigious *banlieues* (suburbs) at bay. Stay or live in central Paris and you are propelled into a maelstrom of gastronomy, fashion, cinema, literature, art…and monuments. History is omnipresent and no ruler – whether king or president – has failed to leave his mark on the city's urban face.

Philosophy, ideas, and culture have always been favourite Parisian preoccupations, but in this *fin de siècle* the momentum is slowing. The population is stagnating as inhabitants flee big-city life for less costly environs. Live here and you spend money: the temptations are multifarious and nothing comes cheap. New buildings proliferated with President Mitterrand's *grands projets* of the 1980s, historic mansions are renovated and state culture monopolises every corner. Some say the city is becoming an asphyxiated museum, but spend a few days here and you cannot fail to be seduced by an enduring beauty, a grandeur and a dynamism that few other capital cities combine.

Café life

Place Saint-Sulpice, in the Latin Quarter

Paris still harbours a fascinating cosmopolitan character. Stroll from one *quartier* to the next and you make a minor global tour, taking in Africa, Asia, the Caribbean and the Arab world in Pigalle, Belleville or the 13th *arrondissement*. Plunge into the heart of the French bourgeois soul in the 7th or 16th *arrondissements*, or sweep up Parisian chic on the Left Bank. Stop at a café terrace to people-watch, read or dream; wander along the *quais* or collapse in a park.

Explore the Right Bank and you feel the capital's commercial pulse. Follow the city's cultural history in any of its numerous museums, catch up on new films at the countless cinemas or dive into a hot nightspot. But above all let the city lead you and do not believe the cliché that Parisians are unfriendly. Its winding streets hold surprises that even the most informative guidebook cannot cover, and it is only off the tourist beat that you encounter the true Parisian spirit.

Incomparable Paris

'Paris is complete, Paris is the ceiling of human kind... Whoever sees Paris thinks he sees the basis of all history with a sky and constellations in between. Paris is synonymous with the cosmos...it has no limits. Paris does more than make the law, it makes fashion. Paris can be stupid if it wants, it sometimes allows itself this luxury... It is more than great, it is immense. Why? Because it dares.'
Victor Hugo, *Les Misérables.*

7

PARIS IN FIGURES

HISTORICAL
(city growth)

- 1851: Paris represented 3% of the French population
- 1921: Paris population was 3 million
- 1925: Exposition des Arts Décoratifs drew 16 million visitors
- 1940: Germans occupying Paris saw only 25% of its inhabitants
- 1954: Paris represented 15% of population
- 1954: 80% of Parisian homes had no bathroom
- 1990: 87% of Parisian homes had a WC

SOCIO-POLITICAL

- 10% of Parisians regularly attend mass
- 45% of Parisians go to the cinema at least once a week
- An estimated 200,000–300,000 are homeless
- An estimated 150,000–400,000 are drug-addicts
- Parisians form 4% of the French population and provide 45% of total income tax revenue
- 53% of Parisians use a car daily, 35% use public transport
- The 1980s per capita cultural budget for Paris was 20 times that of the provinces
- 15% of Parisians are manual workers
- 30% of Parisians are executives or intellectuals
- 20 million tourists visit Paris annually
- 45% of Parisians live alone
- The Louvre had 6.3 million visitors in 1994
- 200,000 Parisian dogs produce 10 tonnes of excrement daily
- 800,000 French regularly consult a psychiatrist
- 90% of French women and 50% of French men use perfume

GEOGRAPHICAL

- 2.1 million inhabitants within the city walls (decreasing)
- 10.6 million inhabitants in the Ile de France (increasing)
- 20,000 inhabitants per sq km and an average of 1.92 per residence
- During July and August over 2 million cars head south
- 600km of underground sewers
- 15,000 restaurants, cafés and clubs

PARIS PEOPLE

JEAN-PAUL GAULTIER

Now in his early forties, Jean-Paul Gaultier is still a prime mover in the fickle French fashion world. After spending his formative years with *haute-couturiers* Pierre Cardin and Jean Patou, in 1979 he created his own label. From his first 'James Bond' collection, through 'Dadism', 'Witches' and 'High-Tech', Gaultier aimed to shock. Costumes for films, mobile furniture, a record, and TV shows in the UK have paralleled his two annual fashion collections.

JOËL ROBUCHON

The man behind innovative Parisian gastronomy may be modest but his star still rises. In 1981 Robuchon took over a restaurant in the 16th *arrondissement*, and has not looked back since, accumulating gastronomy medals, writing books, playing French food ambassador and confirming his status as France's top chef. In 1996 he abandoned his restaurant to become a roving *éminence grise* and front a TV show on channel TF1.

ANNE SINCLAIR

The thinking man's crumpet, chic TV interviewer Anne Sinclair has become the most popular woman in France in the last decade. Steering top personalities through their analysis of the week's events in her one-hour programme, *7 sur 7*, this dark-haired, blue-eyed charmer has managed to extract declarations, confessions, hopes and fears from such key names as Mikhail Gorbachov, Prince Charles, Madonna and François Mitterrand.

PHILIPPE STARCK

Tripod orange-squeezers, chairs with pointed legs, a laughing TV – these are the hallmarks of Starck's design success. A 'Made in France' phenomenon of the 1980s, Starck – gregarious, corpulent and bearded – has presence in the 1990s. Still going strong is his redesign of the nightclub Les Bains Douches, while his latest gimmick is a mail-order house-kit composed of plans, a videotape and a hammer.

Jean-Paul Gaultier

Jacques Chirac

For over 18 years Jacques Chirac, the ebullient mayor of Paris and leader of the Gaullist party (RPR) surveyed the city from his palatial working residence overlooking the Seine, the Hôtel de Ville. With a taste for reading Chinese poetry (in French), he transformed the city's infrastructure and repeatedly clashed with the ruling Socialists until in May 1995, after two previously unsuccessful shots, he was finally elected president of France.

A CHRONOLOGY

c. 200 BC	Celtic tribe of Parisii settles on Ile de la Cité
c. AD 100	Growth of Gallo-Roman city of Lutetia
451	Ste Geneviève saves Paris from Attila the Hun
1100s	Tragic love-affair of Abélard and Héloïse
1163	Building starts on Notre-Dame
1215	University of Paris founded
1358	Royal family installed in Marais and Louvre
1337–1453	Hundred Years War between France and England
1430	Henry VI of England crowned king of France in Notre-Dame
1437	Charles VII regains control of Paris
1572	St Bartholomew's Massacre ignites Wars of Religion
1600s	Paris reorganised; Le Marais developed
1648–52	Civil uprising of La Fronde
1672	Louis XIV moves to Versailles
1700s	Development of Faubourg Saint-Germain
1789	Storming of the Bastille; declaration of Rights of Man
1792	Monarchy abolished; proclamation of the Republic
1793–4	Reign of Terror; Louis XVI beheaded; inauguration of the Musée du Louvre
1804	Napoleon Bonaparte crowned emperor
1800–14	Building of imperial monuments. Founding of Grandes Ecoles; increased centralisation

1830	Bourbons overthrown; Louis-Philippe crowned
1848	Revolution topples Louis-Philippe; Second Republic headed by Napoleon III
1852–70	Baron Haussmann transforms urban Paris
1870–1	Paris besieged by Prussians; civil uprising of the Commune; Republic restored
1889	Eiffel Tower built for Exposition Universelle
1900	Grand and Petit Palais built for Exposition Universelle; first métro line opens
c. 1908	Modernism born in Montmartre with Picasso
1914–18	Paris bombarded by German cannon, Big Bertha
1925	Exposition des Arts Décoratifs introduces art deco style
1940	Nazis occupy Paris
1944	Liberation of Paris led by Général de Gaulle
1954	National funeral for writer Colette
1958	De Gaulle called in to head Fifth Republic
1967	Les Halles market transferred to Rungis
1969	President Georges Pompidou elected
1974	President Valéry Giscard d'Estaing elected
1977	Jacques Chirac elected first mayor of Paris since 1871; Centre Georges Pompidou opens
1981	Election of President Mitterrand initiates *Grands Travaux*
1989	Bicentenary celebrations of the Revolution
1995	Election of President Chirac

PEOPLE & EVENTS FROM HISTORY

*Napoleon Bonaparte
(1769–1821)*

Henri IV

Authoritarian, complex and charismatic, Henri IV (1553–1610) was also Paris's first urban designer. In 1594, after renouncing Protestantism and uttering the legendary words 'Paris is well worth a mass', he triumphantly entered the city as a long-needed unifying force. His reign saw the growth of new industries, a fashion for châteaux and the downfall of the peasant classes. Meanwhile, he instigated the building of Place Royale (Place des Vosges), Place Dauphine and the Pont Neuf, the rise of Le Marais and the planting of 20,000 trees in the Tuileries before losing his life by an assassin's knife.

REVOLUTION

The Revolution of 1789 signalled the end of absolute royal power and the rise of popular democracy. The royal family was forced from Versailles to the Tuileries palace, but in 1792 this in turn was attacked and Louis XVI and Marie-Antoinette were imprisoned and sent to the guillotine. The year 1792–3 marked the high point of the Terror, which was led by Robespierre, himself guillotined in 1794.

NAPOLEON

Napoleon Bonaparte's meteoric rise and fall from power (1800–14) left an indelible mark on the capital. Ambitious reforms included the construction of neo-classical buildings, while his military campaigns made Paris capital of the greatest European empire since Charlemagne. More important was the increased concentration of the nation's culture and government in Paris, something that decentralisation has still not eradicated two centuries later.

OCCUPATION

The scars left by France's Vichy régime were most apparent in Paris, occupied by the Nazis from 1940. Luxury hotels and public buildings were requisitioned, and Communists and Jews were deported in their thousands. After the Allies disembarked in Normandy in June 1944, a week-long insurrection by Parisians opened a path for them into the capital. General Von Cholitz capitulated after disobeying Hitler's orders to blow up the city, and Paris was reborn.

'LE GÉNÉRAL'

De Gaulle's role as one of France's major 20th-century figures started during the Occupation, when he headed the Free French Forces from London, continued with the Liberation and was consolidated when he was called from retirement to solve the divisive Algerian War and head the Fifth Republic in 1958. His rule heralded increased presidential powers, a burgeoning consumer society and the prominence of France within the European Union.

PARIS
how to organise your time

13

ITINERARIES

One of the pleasures of Paris is its compact scale and efficient public transport service. Visiting monuments in the central *arrondissements* is easiest and most scenic on foot and always includes obligatory café stops, but do not hesitate to dive into the métro for a short burst to more distant sights.

Moving between the monuments on Sundays and public holidays from mid-April to late September is facilitated by Balabus, a public bus service that starts at the Gare de Lyon and stops at Saint-Michel, Musée d'Orsay, Louvre, Concorde, Champs-Elysées, Charles de Gaulle-Etoile, Porte Maillot and Neuilly. Services run between 12.30PM and 8PM and the whole trip takes 50 minutes. You can get off to visit a sight near a Balabus stop, then catch the next bus onwards.

An alternative way of travelling around Paris between April and September is by a public river-boat christened 'Batobus'. Fares are paid either per stage or for the entire journey, which starts at the Port de la Bourdonnais by the Eiffel Tower and continues to the Musée d'Orsay, the Pont des Arts (Louvre), Notre-Dame and Hôtel de Ville (Centre Georges Pompidou), and then returns along the same route.

ITINERARY ONE	LATIN QUARTER
Morning	Climb the tower of Notre-Dame (► 43) for a bird's-eye view over the city Walk beside the river to the Sainte-Chapelle (► 39) Cross to Boulevard Saint-Michel and walk up to the Musée de Cluny (► 38) Continue up Boulevard Saint-Michel to the Jardin du Luxembourg (► 37)
Lunch	Relax in the gardens and have lunch in a café near the Panthéon
Afternoon	Walk over to Eglise Saint-Etienne-du-Mont (► 52) Explore the winding streets that lead to the rue Monge Have a look at the Roman Arènes de Lutèce (► 59)
Tea	Walk south towards the Mosquée (► 52) and indulge in a mint tea Cross over to the Jardin des Plantes botanical garden and the Muséum National d'Histoire Naturelle (► 51)

ITINERARY TWO	**STATELY PARIS**
Breakfast	At the Samaritaine (➤ 57)
Morning	Cross Pont Neuf (➤ 55) to the island and take a boat trip along the Seine which returns to the island. Wander along the *quai* at river level to the Musée d'Orsay (➤ 31)
Lunch	Have lunch at the Musée d'Orsay, or walk up rue de Bellechasse and across Boulevard Saint-Germain to the Musée Rodin (➤ 29), with its rose-garden café
Afternoon	Continue to Les Invalides (➤ 28) Visit the Eglise du Dôme (➤ 28) Walk along the esplanade to cross the ornate Pont Alexandre III (➤ 55) Visit the Petit Palais (➤ 27) Explore the Champs-Elysées (➤ 27) Catch bus No 42 down Avenue Montaigne to the Eiffel Tower (➤ 26). Time it for sunset
ITINERARY THREE	**GREEN PARIS**
Morning	Start the day at the Musée Marmottan (➤ 24), then take the métro to Franklin-D Roosevelt Walk down the paths of the Champs-Elysées (➤ 27) to Place de la Concorde (➤ 30) Cross to the Orangerie (➤ 30) Walk through the Tuileries (➤ 56), stopping for a drink at a kiosk
Lunch	Have lunch at the Café Marly (➤ 53) or in the Louvre's underground labyrinth
Afternoon	Visit a section of the Louvre's immense collection (➤ 35) then recover in the gardens of the Palais-Royal (➤ 59) Take bus No 67 from the rue du Louvre to Pigalle, where you can catch the Monmartrobus to the top of Montmartre hill Watch the sun set over Paris from Sacré-Coeur (➤ 33)
Evening	Dine near the lively Place des Abbesses

15

WALKS

INFORMATION

Distance 3km
Time 1–2 hours
Start point Plateau Beaubourg
🚇 H5/6
🚉 Rambuteau, Hôtel de Ville
End point Place des Vosges
🚇 J6
🍴 Café Beaubourg, rue Saint-Martin; Ma Bourgogne, Place des Vosges (➤ 73)

Mère et enfant, *Picasso*

LE MARAIS TO THE PLACE DES VOSGES

After breakfast at the Café Beaubourg walk behind the Centre Georges Pompidou and turn right into the rue Rambuteau, a colourful food-shopping street. Turn left up the rue des Archives with the magnificent turreted Porte de Clisson (1375) rising from the Hôtel de Soubise (1709) on your right. Continue past a monumental fountain (1624) on your left and the Hôtel Guénégaud (1650) – which houses the Musée de la Chasse – diagonally opposite. Keep walking straight on to the rue de Bretagne, where you can rest in the leafy Square du Temple or investigate the leather-clothes market in the Carreau du Temple. Have a coffee near by.

Along the rue de Bretagne, enter the picturesque food and flower market of Les Enfants Rouges (dating from the 1620s), then exit on to the rue Charlot. Walk south past the impressive Cathédrale Sainte-Croix-de-Paris, a former 17th-century convent, to the rue des Quatre-Fils. Turn left, past a new building which houses the National Archives, and continue to the rue Vieille-du-Temple. Circle round the garden of the Hôtel Salé, now home to the Musée Picasso, then continue to the Parc Royal, a small garden which is overlooked by a row of superbly restored 17th-century mansions. Take a look at the courtyard of the Hôtel de Chatillon at 13 rue Payenne, then continue to rue de Sévigné. Pass or be tempted by the fashion offerings of Romeo Gigli at No 46, admire the two mansions of the Musée Carnavalet, then turn left into the rue des Francs-Bourgeois. Carry straight on to the Place des Vosges and stop to have lunch at Ma Bourgogne.

16

PLACE DES VOSGES TO THE LATIN QUARTER

Walk through a passageway at No 9 Place des Vosges to the courtyard of the Hôtel de Sully. Exit on to the rue Saint-Antoine, turn right and right again into the rue de Turenne, then turn left to the charming Place du Marché Sainte-Catherine, good for a coffee-stop on a sunny day. Return to the main road and cross to rue Saint-Paul, lined with antique shops. Further down on the right enter the Village Saint-Paul, a discreetly situated bric-à-brac market, then emerge on the other side into the rue des Jardins Saint-Paul. Here you see the largest remaining section of Philippe-Auguste's city wall. Turn left, then right along the rue de l'Ave Maria to reach the Hôtel de Sens, an exceptional example of 15th-century Gothic architecture. Look at the court-yard and the small formal garden behind the mansion. From here cross the Pont Marie to the Ile Saint-Louis. End your day in the web of Latin Quarter streets across the Seine.

THE SIGHTS

- Place des Vosges
- Village Saint-Paul (➤ 77)
- Philippe-Auguste's city wall
- Hôtel de Sens
- Ile Saint-Louis (➤ 44)

INFORMATION

Distance 2km
Time 1–2 hours
Start point Place des Vosges
🚇 J6
🚇 Bastille, Chemin Vert, Saint-Paul
End point Latin Quarter, around Boulevard Saint-Michel, rue Saint-Jacques
🚇 G/H6/7

Place des Vosges   **17**

EVENING STROLLS

INFORMATION

The Seine
Start point Place du Châtelet
🚇 H6
Ⓜ Châtelet

Bastille
Start point Place de la Bastille
🚇 J/K6
Ⓜ Bastille

The Conciergerie at the Palais de Justice

THE SEINE

Start at Châtelet and walk towards the Louvre along the embankment opposite the illuminated Conciergerie, the Monnaie (Mint) and the Institut de France. At the Louvre make a detour into the Cour Carrée, magnificently lit and often deserted at night. Return to the river, cross the lively Pont des Arts then walk back along the opposite bank, this time with views north of the stately Samaritaine and the Palais de Justice on the Ile de la Cité. Continue towards Saint-Michel, then cross over to Notre-Dame and make your way around the north side of the island, which offers views of the Ile Saint-Louis, the Hôtel de Ville and the Gothic Tour Saint-Jacques towering over the Place du Châtelet.

BASTILLE

From the Place de la Bastille walk up the rue de la Roquette until the road forks. Turn right along the bustling pedestrian street of rue de Lappe, which is packed with bars, nightclubs and restaurants (keep a look out for No 71, a fine 18th-century house). Then turn left into the rue de Charonne. Pass art galleries and more bars before cutting back to the rue de la Roquette via the rue Keller. Notre-Dame de l'Espérance looms on your right, and at No 68 there is a fountain (1839). Back at the fork turn right along rue Daval and cross two boulevards to reach rue du Pas de la Mule, following it to reach the Place des Vosges.

ORGANISED SIGHTSEEING

WALKING TOURS

CAISSE DES MONUMENTS HISTORIQUES ET DES SITES

Offers a daily programme of walking tours with qualified lecturers.

✉ 62 rue Saint-Antoine 75004 ☎ 01 44 61 21 50/51 🚇 Bastille, Saint-Paul 🏷 Moderate

The **Ville de Paris** (municipality) offers guided tours to the Parc de Bagatelle, the Parc André Citroën and the Père Lachaise, Montmartre and Passy cemeteries.

☎ 01 40 67 97 00. Recorded information: 01 40 71 76 47

BOAT TRIPS

BATEAUX PARISIENS TOUR EIFFEL

✉ Rive Gauche, Port de la Bourdonnais ☎ 01 44 11 33 44 🕐 Mon–Thu 10–6; Fri–Sun 10–9 🚇 Trocadéro 🏷 Very expensive

BATEAUX VEDETTES DU PONT-NEUF

Classic one-hour trip along the Seine.

✉ Square du Vert Galant 75001 ☎ 01 46 33 98 38 🕐 Daily 10–7 🚇 Pont Neuf 🏷 Expensive

CANAUXRAMA

Three-hour canal trip (part underground) between the Bastille and the Bassin de la Villette. Booking essential.

✉ Bassin de la Villette, 13 Quai de la Loire 75019 ☎ 01 42 39 15 00 🕐 Departures at 9:30 and 2:45 from Bassin de la Villette; 9:45 and 2:30 from the Port de l'Arsenal, Bastille 🚇 Jaurès or Bastille 🏷 Very expensive

BICYCLE TOURS

PARIS BIKE

Paris and further afield on VTT (mountain) bikes.

✉ 83 rue Daguerre 75013 ☎ 01 30 51 87 64 🕐 Three-hour circuits and weekend trips 🚇 Denfert-Rochereau 🏷 Expensive

PARIS À VÉLO

✉ 9 rue Jacques Coeur 75004 ☎ 01 48 87 60 01 🕐 Short and long trips 🚇 Bastille 🏷 Expensive

---

Paris's canals

Cruising Paris's canals offers a more idiosyncratic view the city than the usual Seine trip. The revamped Arsenal dock at the Bastille (1806) is the kick-off for an underground vaulted passage which re-emerges at the Canal Saint-Martin. Chestnut trees, swing bridges, locks, the Hôtel du Nord (of celluloid fame) and modern apartment blocks lead to the Bassin de la Villette, with its famous Rotonde (built by Ledoux in 1789). From here, the Canal de l'Ourcq leads to the Parc de la Villette and then continues eastwards for a further 108km.

EXCURSIONS

CHÂTEAU AND PARK OF VERSAILLES

Few tourists fail to visit Versailles, the ultimate symbol of French grandeur and sophistication, and the backdrop to the death throes of the monarchy. In 1661, when Louis XIV announced his intention of moving his court to this deserted swamp, it was to create a royal residence, seat of government and home to French nobility. Building continued until his death in 1715, by which time the 100ha park had been tamed to perfection by Le Nôtre. Hundreds of statues, follies and fountains, and the royal love nests of the Grand and Petit Trianon relieve the formal symmetry, while rowing-boats, bicycles and a minitrain now offer instant relief from history. Inside the château, visit the Grands Appartements (the official court and entertainment halls), which include the staggeringly ornate Hall of Mirrors with painted ceilings by Lebrun. The Petits Appartements (the royal living quarters) display France's most priceless examples of 18th-century decoration and may be visited by guided tour only.

The Latona fountain, Versailles

VAUX-LE-VICOMTE

About 50km south-east of Paris lies the inspiration for Versailles, a château erected in 1656 by Louis XIV's ambitious regent and minister of finance, Nicolas Fouquet, who employed the nation's most talented artists and craftsmen. Five years later, a château-warming party of

The lily pond at Giverny

extravagant proportions provoked Louis XIV's envy and resulted in the arrest and imprisonment of Fouquet for embezzlement. Today, the interior and magnificent grounds have been entirely restored and include the Musée des Equipages (horse-drawn carriages) in the stables. Inside the château, resplendent with Lebrun's painted ceilings, do not miss the rich Chambre du Roi. In front of the château's neo-classical façade stretch terraces, lawns, fountains and statues, these ending at a canal. If you have time, continue your stroll in the woods beyond.

GIVERNY

This small Normandy village is famous for one reason – Claude Monet. The painter lived in the village from 1883 until his death in 1926, inspiring a local artists' colony and producing some of Impressionism's most famous and startling canvases. His carefully tended garden with its Japanese-style lily pond gradually became his sole inspiration, and was as important to him as his painting. Only reproductions of his works are displayed here, but the colourfully painted house, his personal collection of Japanese prints and the beautiful garden together offer a wonderful day out. May–June, when the borders are a riot of colour, is the best time for the flowers.

Le Petit Trianon

The Petit Trianon, the jewel in the crown of French neo-classical architecture, was built for Louis XV's mistress, Madame du Barry, and later presented by Louis XVI to his wife, Marie-Antoinette (who was to utter the inept words 'let them eat cake' from her royal chambers as the angry mob below clamoured for bread). In a pursuit of the simple life, Marie-Antoinette transformed the grounds into a 'wild' park, complete with a make-believe village where she tended sheep.

21

WHAT'S ON

Information on current events is best found in *Pariscope*, an inexpensive weekly listings magazine (out on Wednesday) which covers everything from concerts to cinema, theatre, sports and nightclubs; it has a useful section in English. *Figaroscope* comes with *Le Figaro* on Wednesdays and also offers a good round-up of current events.

JANUARY	*America Stakes*: at Vincennes racecourse
FEBRUARY	*National Rugby Tournament*
MARCH	*International Jumping*: at Palais Omnisports de Paris Bercy
APRIL	*International Paris Fair*: stands promoting gastronomy, tourism and publications from all over the world
MAY	*Labour Day* (1 May): sees endless processions, thousands of bouquets of symbolic lilies of the valley and no newspapers
	Armistice Day (8 May)
JUNE	*Fête de la Musique* (midsummer's night): crowds spring to life during this government-sponsored event, which schedules major rock and world-music bands
	Course des Garçons de Café (late June): over 500 waiters and waitresses career along the streets, each armed with tray, bottle and glasses
JULY	*Bastille Day* (14 July): number one on the French festival calendar – celebrates the 1789 storming of the Bastille. Fireworks and street-dances take over on the evening of 13 July, while the 14th itself is devoted to a military parade on the Champs-Elysées
AUGUST	Annual exodus and *Fête des quartiers*: outdoor concerts and street theatre
SEPTEMBER	*Fête à Neu-Neu*: a fair in the Bois de Boulogne
	Festival d'Automne à Paris (mid-September until the end of December): music, theatre and dance performances are staged throughout the city
OCTOBER	*Foire International d'Art Contemporain*: Paris's biggest modern art fair, at the Grand Palais
NOVEMBER	*Beaujolais Nouveau* (third Thursday in November): liberal amounts of wine are drunk when the first bottles hit Paris
	Antiques fair: at Pelouse d'Auteuil, Place de la Porte de Passy
DECEMBER	*Paris International Boat Show*: at the Porte de Versailles

PARIS's
top 25 sights

The sights are shown on the maps on the inside front cover and inside back cover, numbered **1–25** *from west to east across the city*

1

MUSÉE MARMOTTAN

INFORMATION

- ➕ B6
- ✉ 2 rue Louis-Boilly 75016
- ☎ 01 42 24 07 02
- 🕐 Tue–Sun 10–5:30
- 🚇 La Muette
- 🚌 32
- 🚉 RER Line C Boulainvilliers
- 💶 Expensive
- ↔ Bois de Boulogne (➤ 56)

❝*One of the few incentives to get me out into the residential 16th* **arrondissement** *is the Marmottan, where a mesmerising collection of Monet paintings makes a welcome escape from the often colourless Parisian landscape.***❞**

Rich donations This often overlooked treasure of Parisian culture offers an eclectic collection built up over the years from the original donation of Renaissance and First Empire paintings and furniture given to the nation by the art-historian Paul Marmottan in 1932. His discreetly elegant 19th-century mansion, furnished with Renaissance tapestries and sculptures and Napoleonic furniture, was later given an extra boost by an exceptional donation from Michel Monet. This included 65 works by his father Claude Monet, the Impressionist painter, as well as the stunning Wildenstein collection of 230 illustrated manuscripts of the 13th to 16th centuries. Works by Monet's contemporaries Gauguin, Renoir, Pissarro, Sisley, Berthe Morisot and Gustave Caillebotte add to the Impressionist focus, but it is above all Monet's luminous canvases of dappled irises, wisteria and water-lilies, dating from his last years at Giverny, that are memorable.

Shame It happens even to the best of museums, but when nine major paintings were stolen from the Marmottan in 1985 it caused acute embarrassment, not least because the booty included Monet's seminal work, *Impression – soleil levant,* which gave the movement its name. Five years later, after a police operation on a world-wide scale, the plundered paintings were discovered in Corsica. They are now on display once again, needless to say under greatly increased security.

Top: Impression – soleil levant, *Monet*

PALAIS DE CHAILLOT

"With its majestic wings curving towards the Eiffel Tower across the Seine and its monumental presence, the Palais de Chaillot impresses. But it also has a human aspect: roller-skating heroes, mime-artists and Sunday promenaders."

Attractions The 1937 Exposition Universelle instigated the Palais de Chaillot's columns, these punctuated with bronze statues which overlook terraces and fountains. This spectacular art deco wrapping contains four museums, a theatre and the Cinémathèque Française. The west wing houses the Musée de l'Homme and the Musée de la Marine, the former catering to anthropological leanings and the latter to maritime and naval interests. A newly converted gallery at the Musée de l'Homme houses temporary thematic exhibitions, while the main collection gathers dust upstairs awaiting imminent renovation. On the top floor is the Salon de la Musique, which displays some 500 'world' musical instruments used for Sunday concerts.

Illusions In the building's east wing nestles an extra-ordinary museum, the Musée des Monuments Français, conceived by the 19th-century medievalist architect, Viollet-le-Duc. Full-scale replicas and casts of French architectural fea-

An exhibit in the marine museum

tures from pre-Roman times to the 19th century include gargoyles, frescoes, stained glass, statues and even a fountain. More replicas of reality can be found in the adjoining Musée du Cinéma, which traces the evolution of film-making through early movie cameras, sets and costumes.

HIGHLIGHTS

- Napoleon's imperial barge
- *Ports de France*, Vernet
- *Le Valmy*
- African frescoes
- Javanese *gamelan* orchestra
- King Béhanzin
- Reproduction of Saint-Savin-sur-Gartempe
- Baroque fountain
- Fritz Lang's robot
- Rudolf Valentino costume

INFORMATION

- ✚ D5
- ✉ Place du Trocadéro 75016
- ☎ Marine: 01 45 53 31 70.
  Homme: 01 44 05 72 72.
  Monuments: 01 44 05 39 10.
  Cinema: 01 45 53 74 39
- ◷ Marine: Wed–Mon 10–6.
  Homme: Wed–Mon 9:45–5:15.
  Monuments: Wed–Mon 10–6.
  Cinéma: by guided tour only, Wed–Sun 10, 11, 2, 3, 4, 5 (phone to book)
- 🍴 Le Totem restaurant in the west wing
- Ⓜ Trocadéro
- 🚌 22, 30, 32, 63
- ♿ Few
- 💲 Moderate
- ↔ Musée d'Art Moderne de la Ville de Paris (➤ 50)
- ❓ Guided tours of Marine on request; ethnological films at Homme Sat–Sun 2:30

3

TOUR EIFFEL

HIGHLIGHTS

- Panoramic views
- Bust of Gustave Eiffel

DID YOU KNOW?

- Weight: over 7,000 tonnes
- Made of 15,000 iron sections
- Height: 320m
- Top platform at 276m
- 1,652 steps to the top
- 50 tonnes of paint needed to repaint it
- 370 suicides

INFORMATION

- ✚ D6
- ✉ Champ de Mars 75007
- ☎ 01 44 11 23 45
- 🕐 Sep–Jun daily 9AM–11PM. Jul–Aug daily 9AM–midnight
- 🍴 La Belle France (1st floor ☎ 01 45 55 20 04); Jules Verne (2nd floor ☎ 01 45 55 61 44)
- 🚇 Bir-Hakeim
- 🚌 42, 82
- 🚉 RER Line C, Tour Eiffel
- ♿ Very good (to 2nd floor)
- 👆 Very expensive; stairs cheap
- ↔ Les Invalides (➤ 28)

" *The Eiffel Tower could easily be a cliché but it isn't. The powerful silhouette of Gustave Eiffel's marvel of engineering still makes a stirring sight, especially at night when its delicate, lace-like iron structure comes to the fore.* **"**

Glittering feat Built in a record two years for the 1889 Exposition Universelle, the controversial Eiffel Tower was never intended to be a permanent feature of the city. However, in 1910 it was finally saved for posterity, so preparing the way for today's 4 million annual visitors. Avoid long queues for the lift by visiting the tower at night, when it fully lives up to its romantic image and provides a glittering spectacle – whether the 292,000-watt illumination of the 'staircase to infinity' itself, or the carpet of nocturnal Paris unfolding at its feet.

Violent reactions Gustave Eiffel was a master of cast-iron structures, his prolific output including hundreds of factories, churches, railway viaducts and bridges over four continents. His 320m tower attracted vociferous opposition, but his genius was vindicated by the fact that it sways no more

than 12cm in high winds and remained the world's highest structure for 40 years. Eiffel kept an office here until his death in 1923; from it he may have seen Comte de Lambert circle above in a flying-machine in 1909, or a less fortunate Icarus plummet to his death from the parapet in 1912.

CHAMPS-ELYSÉES & ARC DE TRIOMPHE

"Like me, you may not be enamoured of fast-food outlets and airline offices, both major features of this once-glamorous avenue. But a recent face-lift has upgraded it, and nothing can change the magnificent east–west perspective."

Slow start It was Marie de Médicis, wife of Henri IV, who first made this a fashionable driveway in 1616, but it was the celebrated landscape designer André Le Nôtre who contributed to its name – Elysian Fields – by planting alleys of trees and gardens. The heyday came in 1824 when new pavements and fountains made it the most fashionable prom-enading spot in Paris, with cafés and restaurants catering for a well-heeled clientele. Crowning the cake was the Arc de Triomphe (► 57), commissioned by Napoleon, while the 1900 Exposition Universelle added the glass and iron domes of the Grand Palais (which includes the Palais de la Découverte) and the Petit Palais at the lower end.

Parades Despite being dominated by commer-cial and tourist facilities, the Champs-Elysées remains the symbolic focal point for national ceremonies, whether the traditional 14 July mili-tary parade, Armistice Day's wreath-laying at the Arc de Triomphe or the fast-pedalling *grande finale* of the Tour de France. A recent highlight was the 1989 Bicentenary procession, when Jessye Norman led a spectacular host of swaying performers down to the Place de la Concorde.

Luxury These days the Champs-Elysées may be dominated by car showrooms, but plush cinemas, up-market shops and one or two fash-ionable watering-holes still remain to tempt those who want to see and be seen.

HIGHLIGHTS

- Arc de Triomphe
- Rude's 'Marseillaise' sculpture on Arc de Triomphe
- L'Etoile
- Bluebell Girls at Lido
- Fouquets restaurant
- Palais de l'Elysée
- Ledoyen restaurant
- Grand Palais
- Petit Palais
- Philatelists' market

INFORMATION

- ✚ D4
- ✉ Champs-Elysées 75008
- ☎ Grand Palais: 01 44 13 17 17. Petit Palais: 01 42 65 12 73. Découverte: 01 40 74 81 82
- 🕐 Grand Palais: Wed–Mon 10–8. Petit Palais: Tue–Sun 10–5:40. Palais de la Découverte: Tue–Sat 9:30–6; Sun 10–7
- 🍴 Grand Palais: average cafe-teria. Cafés and restaurants on Champs-Elysées
- 🚇 Charles de Gaulle-Etoile, Georges V, Franklin-D Roosevelt, Champs-Elysées-Clémenceau
- 🚌 32, 42, 73
- ♿ Good
- 💰 Moderate to expensive
- ↔ Place de la Concorde (► 30)
- ❓ Photo library and scientific films in Palais de la Découverte

5

LES INVALIDES

HIGHLIGHTS

- 196m façade
- Sword and armour of François I
- Salle Orientale
- Napoleon's stuffed horse
- *Emperor Napoleon*, Ingres
- Galerie des Plans-Reliefs
- Napoleon's tomb
- Dome
- 17th-century organ
- A Renault light tank

INFORMATION

- ✚ E6
- ✉ Esplanade des Invalides 75007
- ☎ Musée de l'Armée, 01 44 42 37 67
- 🕐 Oct–Mar daily 10–5. Apr–Sep daily 10–6
- Ⓜ La Tour Maubourg, Invalides, Varenne
- 🚌 28, 49, 69, 82, 92
- Ⓡ RER Line C Invalides
- ♿ Good
- 💷 Expensive
- ↔ Musée Rodin (► 29)
- ❓ Guided tours on request ☎ 01 45 51 95 05; films on World Wars I and II

"The gilded dome rising above the Hôtel des Invalides reminds me of the pomp and glory of France's two greatest promoters – the Sun King, who built Les Invalides, and the power-hungry Napoleon Bonaparte, who is entombed there."

Glory The vast, imposing edifice of Les Invalides was built to house invalided soldiers, and it continues to accommodate a handful today. Its classical façade and majestic Cour d'Honneur date from the 1670s, with the ornate Eglise du Dôme completed in 1706 and the long grassy esplanade established soon after. Home to military institutions, Les Invalides is also a memorial to the endless battles and campaigns that have marked French history and which are extensively illustrated in the Musée de l'Armée. Here you can trace the evolution of warfare from early days to World War II, and there are daily screenings of war films.

The Cour d'Honneur

Tombs There are more relics inside the Eglise Saint-Louis, where tattered enemy standards hang despondently from cornices, but it is above all the baroque cupolas, arches, columns and sculptures of the Eglise du Dôme that highlight France's military achievements and heroes. Tombs of generals fill the chapels while the circular crypt contains Napoleon's grandiose sarcophagus (which incorporates six successive layers), guarded by 12 statues, symbols of his military campaigns.

MUSÉE RODIN

❝As a complete antidote to the military might of Les Invalides, wander into the enchanting Musée Rodin, often forgotten by Parisians. This surprisingly peaceful enclave lifts you out of the hurly-burly of the boulevards into another sphere.**❞**

Hard times This rococo mansion, built for a prosperous wig-maker in 1730, has a chequered history. One owner (Maréchal de Biron) was sent to the guillotine, and the house has been used successively as a dance-hall, convent, school and as artists' studios. Rodin lived here from 1908 until his death in 1917, with such neighbours as the poet Rainer Maria Rilke and dancer Isadora Duncan. In 1919 the house was transformed into a museum.

Sculpture The elegant, luminous interior houses the collection of works which Rodin left to the nation on his death in 1917. It ranges from his early academic sketches to the later water colours, and displays many of his most celebrated white marble and bronze sculptures, including *The Kiss*. There are busts of the composer Mahler, the suffragette Eva Fairfax and Victor Hugo to name but a few, as well as a series of studies of Balzac in paunchy splendour. Alongside the Rodins are works by his contemporaries, in particular his tragic mistress and model, Camille Claudel, as well as Eugène Carrière, Munch, Renoir, Monet and Van Gogh. Rodin's furniture and antiques complete this exceptional collection.

Retreat The museum's private gardens are Paris's third largest and contain several major sculptures, a pond, flowering shrubs, benches for a quiet read, a converted chapel used for temporary exhibitions and an open-air café.

HIGHLIGHTS

- Les Bourgeois de Calais
- La Penseur
- La Porte de l'Enfer
- Le Baiser
- La Main de Dieu
- Saint Jean Baptiste
- Adam et Eve
- Ugolin
- Le Père Tanguy, Van Gogh
- Original staircase

INFORMATION

- F6
- 77 rue de Varenne 75007
- 01 47 05 01 34
- Winter: Tue–Sun 9:30–4:45. Summer: Tue–Sun 9:30–5:45
- Peaceful garden café
- Varenne
- 69
- Good
- Moderate
- Les Invalides (➤ 28)

PLACE DE LA CONCORDE

DID YOU KNOW?

- The Egyptian obelisk weighs 230 tonnes
- 133 people were trampled to death here in 1770
- 1,300 heads were guillotined here in 1793–5

INFORMATION

- F5
- Place de la Concorde 75008
- Jeu de Paume: 01 47 03 12 50.
  Orangerie: 01 42 97 48 16
- Jeu de Paume: Tue noon–9:30; Wed–Fri noon–7; Sat–Sun 10–7. Orangerie: Wed–Mon 9:45–5:15
- Small designer café in Jeu de Paume
- Concorde
- 24, 42, 52, 72, 73, 84, 94
- Jeu de Paume: excellent Orangerie: none
- Moderate to expensive
- Champs-Elysées & Arc de Triomphe (➤ 27), Jardin des Tuileries (➤ 56)

"As you stand in this noisy traffic-choked square it is hard to imagine the crowds baying for the deaths of Marie-Antoinette and Louis XVI, who were both guillotined here at the height of the Terror of the French Revolution."

Chop-chop This pulsating square was initially laid out in 1775 to accommodate a statue of King Louis XV. Under the new name of the Place de la Révolution it then witnessed the mass executions of the French Revolution, and was finally renamed the Place de la Concorde in 1795 as revolutionary zeal abated. In the 19th century, Guillaume Coustou's *Chevaux de Marly* were erected at the base of the Champs-Elysées (those you see today are reproductions, the originals now being housed in the Louvre). Crowning the centre of the Concorde is a 3,000-year-old Egyptian obelisk overlooking eight symbolic statues of French cities. Dodging the traffic to have a closer look is to dice with death, but plans to ease the pedestrian's lot are currently under consideration.

Grandeur To the north, bordering the rue Royale, stand the colonnaded Hôtel Crillon (on the left) and the matching Hôtel de la Marine (right), both relics from pre-Revolutionary days. The rue Royale itself, with its luxury establishments, leads to the Madeleine. The eastern side of the Concorde is dominated by two public art galleries: the Jeu de Paume (by rue de Rivoli), which displays contemporary art exhibitions; and the Orangerie (nearer the river), famous for its impressive basement panels of Monet's *Water Lilies* and rather second-rate Impressionist paintings. Visible across the bridge to the south is the Palais Bourbon, home to the Assemblée Nationale (French parliament).

MUSÉE D'ORSAY

❝*You'll either love or hate this conversion of a turn-of-the-century railway station, but whatever your view its art collections, covering the years 1848–1914, are a must for anyone interested in the output of this crucial period.*❞

Monolithic When this museum finally opened in 1986 controversy ran high: Gae Aulenti's heavy stone structures lay unhappily under Laloux's delicate iron and glass shell, built as a railway terminus in 1900. But the collections redeem this *faux pas*, offering a solid overview of the momentous period from Romanticism to Fauvism. Ignore the monolithic mezzanine blocks and, after exploring the 19th-century

The Church at Auvers, *Van Gogh*

paintings, sculptures and decorative arts on the ground floor, take the front escalator to the upper level. Here the Pont-Aven, Impressionist and Nabis schools are displayed along with the giants of French art – Cézanne, Monet, Renoir, Van Gogh, Degas, Sisley and Pissaro. And don't miss the views from the outside terrace and café behind the station clock at the top.

To the ball The middle level is devoted to painting (Symbolism and Naturalism) and sculpture from 1870 to 1914, and it includes works by Rodin, Bourdelle and Maillol. In the spectacular ballroom hang paintings by Gérôme and Bouguereau.

HIGHLIGHTS

- *Olympia*, Manet
- *Déjeuner sur l'Herbe*, Manet
- *Orphée*, Gustave Moreau
- *La Mère*, Whistler
- *L'Angélus du Soir*, Millet
- *La Cathédrale de Rouen*, Monet
- *L'Absinthe*, Degas
- *La Chambre à Arles*, Van Gogh
- *Femmes de Tahiti*, Gauguin
- Chair by Charles Rennie Mackintosh

INFORMATION

- ✚ F6
- ✉ 1 rue de Bellechasse 75007
- ☎ 01 40 49 48 14; 01 40 49 48 48
- 🕐 Tue–Sun 10–5:45, except Thu 10–9:30
- 🍴 Café des Hauteurs for good snacks; plush restaurant/tea-room in ballroom
- 🚇 Solférino
- 🚌 24, 68, 69
- 🚉 RER Line C Musée d'Orsay
- ♿ Excellent
- 💷 Expensive
- ↔ Musée du Louvre (➤ 35)
- ❓ Audio and guided tours; pedagogical activities, concerts and lectures

TOP 25

9

OPÉRA DE PARIS

HIGHLIGHTS

- Grand Escalier
- Grand Foyer
- *Apollo*, Millet
- Façade
- Lamp-bearers

DID YOU KNOW?

- Garnier's design was selected from 171 others
- The total surface area of the building is 11,000sq m
- The auditorium holds 2,200 spectators
- The stage accommodates over 450 performers

INFORMATION

- G4
- Place de l'Opéra 75009
- Monument: 01 40 01 19 70.
  Bookings: 01 44 73 13 00.
  Museum: 01 47 42 07 02
- Daily 10–4:30
- Bar open during shows
- Opéra
- 20, 21, 22, 27, 29, 42, 52, 53, 66, 68, 81, 95
- RER Auber
- Few, call for appointment
- Moderate
- Place de la Concorde (► 30)
- Guided tours daily at 1PM except Mon; exhibitions

"I find it hard to take this ornate wedding cake of a building seriously, but the sumptuous and riotous details that decorate every surface are in fact the perfect epitaph to the frenetic architectural activities of the Second Empire."

Past glory When Charles Garnier's opera house was inaugurated in 1875 it marked the end of Haussmann's ambitious urban face-lift and announced the socio-cultural build-up to the Belle Epoque, with Nijinsky and Diaghilev's Ballets Russes as later highlights. Today, the Salle Garnier still stages dance and opera, although many prestigious operatic performances have been switched to the Opéra Bastille. In 1994–5 it was closed for total renovation to counter the comfort of Opéra Bastille. Rudolf Nureyev was director of the Paris Ballet here between 1983 and 1989, and this was where he first danced in the West. The brilliant dancer Patrick Dupond has steered the national ballet company fairly traditionally since 1990.

Dazzle Competing with a series of provocative lamp-bearing statues, the Palais Garnier's extravagant façade of arches, winged horses, friezes and columns topped by a copper-green dome leads into a majestic foyer. This is dominated by the Grand Escalier, dripping with balconies and chandeliers, in turn sweeping upwards to the Grand Foyer and its gilded mirrors, marble, murals and Murano glass. Do not miss the equally ornate auditorium, with its dazzling gold-leaf decorations and red-velvet seats, or Chagall's incongruous false ceiling, painted in 1964. The Opéra is open outside rehearsals (your best bet is 1–2PM); to visit, enter through Riccardo Pedruzzi's library and the museum of operatic memorabilia.

SACRÉ-COEUR

❝*Few people would admit it, but the high point of a trip up here is not the basilica itself but the stunning views. You can't, however, forget that Sacré-Coeur was built in honour of the 58,000 dead of the Franco–Prussian War.*❞

Weighty Although construction started in 1875, it was not until 1914 that this white neo-Romanesque-Byzantine edifice was completed, partly due to the problems of building foundations in the quarry-riddled hill of Montmartre. Priests still work in relays to maintain the tradition of perpetual prayer for forgiveness of the horrors of war and for the massacre of some 20,000 Communards by government troops.

Byzantine mosaic of Christ, chancel vault

The square bell-tower was an afterthought and houses one of the world's heaviest bells, La Savoyarde, which weighs in at 19 tonnes. The stained-glass windows are replacements for those that were shattered by enemy bombs in 1944.

Panoramas This unmistakable feature of the Paris skyline magnetises the crowds either by funicular or via the steep steps of the terraced garden. Dawn and dusk offer sparkling panoramas over the city, especially from the exterior terrace of the dome, the second-highest point in Paris after the Eiffel Tower (access is from the left-hand side of the basilica). Just to the east of Sacré-Coeur is the diminutive Saint-Pierre, a much reworked though charming church which is all that remains of the Benedictine abbey of Montmartre founded in 1133.

HIGHLIGHTS

- La Savoyarde bell
- View from the dome
- Mosaic of Christ
- Treasure of Sacré-Coeur
- Bronze doors at Saint-Pierre
- Stained-glass gallery
- Statue of Christ
- Statue of Virgin Mary and Child
- The funicular ride from Abbesses métro station

INFORMATION

- ✚ H3
- ✉ 35 rue Chevalier de la Barre 75018
- ☎ 01 53 41 89 00
- 🕐 Basilica: daily 7AM–11PM. Dome and crypt: Apr–Sep daily 9–7. Oct–Mar daily 9–6
- 🚇 Abbesses, then funicular
- 🚌 Montmartrobus from Pigalle or Abbesses
- ♿ Few
- 💰 Basilica: free. Dome and crypt: cheap
- ↔ Montmartre Village (rue Lepic, Vineyard of Montmartre, Place des Abbesses)

11

MUSÉE DES ARTS DÉCORATIFS

HIGHLIGHTS

- Sculpted wood panels
- Reveillon wallpaper designs
- Bronze and wood cradle
- Dufour Leroy wallpaper
- Empress Joséphine's tea service
- Georges Hoentschell woodwork
- Jeanne Lanvin's apartment
- Glass radiator
- Martin Szekely *chaise-longue*
- Toy collection

INFORMATION

- ✚ G5
- ✉ 107 rue de Rivoli 75001
- ☎ 01 44 55 57 50
- 🕐 Wed–Sat 12:30–6; Sun noon–6
- Ⓜ Palais-Royal/Musée du Louvre
- 🚌 21, 27, 39, 48, 67, 69, 72, 81
- ♿ Excellent
- 💷 Moderate
- ↔ Musée du Louvre (➤ 35)

Top: Jeanne Lanvin's bedroom by A A Rateau (1920–2)

> **"**This uncrowded museum is one of my favourites for its discreet, old-fashioned atmosphere and idiosyncratic collections. These may not necessarily be valuable, but they offer a clear view of developments in interior design and decoration.**"**

The collection Tucked away in the north-west wing of the Louvre, this rather oddly arranged museum houses five floors of predominantly French furniture, furnishings and *objets d'art* from the Middle Ages through rococo to the present. It was founded early this century by an association of designers whose aim was to collect and exhibit 'beauty in function', and it certainly lives up to its role. Subsequent donations have greatly enriched the collection, including the contents of the former Musée de la Publicité, thus adding graphic arts to the list. Extensive renovation is under way, so closing some sections until 1999.

What to see The museum is arranged chronologically. The ground floor is devoted to a fascinating collection of 20th-century design, ranging from Le Corbusier to Nikki de St Phalle and Philippe Starck, with superb rooms devoted to art nouveau and art deco as well as temporary exhibitions. Make sure you do not miss the excellent specialist bookshop and small designer gift shop at the entrance. The upper floors display medieval and Renaissance pieces, with better coverage of Louis XIII, Louis XIV, Louis XV, Empire, Restoration, Louis Philippe and Second Empire furnishings, some of which are arranged in reconstructed décors. On the third floor a changing exhibition displays toys throughout the centuries beside an outstanding collection of dolls. Top-floor collections of wallpaper, glass and graphic arts can be viewed only by appointment.

12

MUSÉE DU LOUVRE

"Nocturnal lighting transforms the Louvre's glass pyramid entrance into a gigantic cut diamond – just a foretaste of the treasures contained within. It is hard to ignore the state-of-the-art renovation, but that is just the icing on the cake."

The world's largest museum Few visitors bypass this palatial museum, but definitions of personal interest need to be made beforehand as mere wandering could become a lifetime's occupation. Since 1981 the Louvre has been undergoing a radical transformation which crowns six centuries of eventful existence and which will be completed in 1997. Originally a medieval castle, it first took shape as an art gallery under François I, eager to display his Italian loot, but it was Catherine de Médicis who extended it to become a palace in 1578. After escaping the excesses of the Revolutionary mob, the Louvre became a people's museum in 1793 and was later enlarged and enriched by Napoleon I.

Mona Lisa,
Leonardo da Vinci

Art fortress The vast collection of some 30,000 exhibits is arranged on three floors in three wings: Sully (east), Richelieu (north) and Denon (south), while beneath the elegant Cour Carrée lie the keep and dungeons of the original medieval fortress. Do not miss the two spectacular skylit halls flanking the passageway from Palais-Royal, which display monumental French sculptures, nor the tasteful commercial attractions in the central marble hall.

HIGHLIGHTS

- Palace of Khorsabad
- Egyptian scribe
- Glass pyramid entrance, designed by I M Pei
- *Bataille de San Romano,* Uccello
- *Mona Lisa,* Leonardo da Vinci
- *La Dentellière,* Vermeer
- *Le Radeau de la Méduse,* Géricault
- *Vénus de Milo*
- *Gabrielle d'Estrées et Une des ses Soeurs,* Ecole de Fontainebleau
- Cour Carrée at night

INFORMATION

- ⊞ G5
- ✉ 99 rue de Rivoli 75001
- ☎ 01 40 20 53 17.
  Recorded information: 01 40 20 51 51.
  Auditorium: 01 40 20 51 86
- 🕐 Thu–Sun 9–6; Mon and Wed 9AM–10PM
- 🍴 Wide selection of restaurants and cafés
- Ⓜ Palais-Royal/Musée du Louvre
- 🚌 21, 27, 39, 48,67, 68, 69, 72, 75, 76, 81, 95
- ♿ Excellent
- 💷 Very expensive until 3PM, moderate after 3PM and Sun
- ↔ Musée des Arts Décoratifs (▶ 34), Musée d'Orsay (▶ 31)
- ❓ Audio and digital tours; regular lectures, films, concerts in auditorium

35

13

GALERIES VIVIENNE & COLBERT

DID YOU KNOW?

- Explorer Bougainville lived here
- Revolutionary Simón Bolivar lived here
- Crook-turned-cop Vidocq lived here in the 1840s

INFORMATION

- ✚ G5
- ✉ Galerie Vivienne, Galerie Colbert 75002
- 🎫 Gate at 5 rue de la Banque is permanently open
- 🍴 A Priori Thé (➤ 72); Le Grand Colbert (➤ 71)
- 🚇 Bourse, Palais-Royal/Musée du Louvre
- 🚌 29
- ♿ Good
- 🎟 Free
- ↔ Jardin du Palais-Royal (➤ 59)

The mosaic floor (top) and the bronze statue (right) in the Galerie Vivienne

"These connecting 19th-century passages, with their original mosaic floors and neo-classical decoration, are one of my favourite places for people-watching and offer a complete contrast to the fashionable buzz of neighbouring streets."

Shopping arcades Between the late 18th and early 19th centuries the Right Bank included a network of 140 covered passageways – the fashionable shopping-malls of the time. Today there are fewer than 30, of which the Galeries Vivienne and Colbert are perhaps the best known, strategically squeezed in between the Bibliothèque Nationale and the Place des Victoires. Bookworms and fashion-victims cross paths in this elegant, skylit setting lined with potted palms, where there is also the occasional fashion show. It is perfect for a rainy day browse.

Hive of interest The Galerie Vivienne (1823) opens on to three different streets, while the parallel Galerie Colbert (1826) has its own entrances. Colbert is now an annexe of the Bibliothèque Nationale, and regular exhibitions (prints, photos, theatre accessories) and concerts are held in its galleries and auditorium. Galerie Vivienne is commercial in spirit: this is where you can track down Jean-Paul Gaultier's eccentric shop, designer watches, antiquarian or one-off artists' books, contemporary design, fine wines, intriguing toys or simply sit sipping exotic tea beneath the skylight, watching the world go by.

JARDIN DU LUXEMBOURG

" *Despite the crowds, these gardens are serene in all weathers and are the epitome of French landscaping. Their occupants present an idealised image of an unhurried Parisian existence far from the daily truth of noise and traffic.* **"**

Layout Radiating from the large octagonal pond in front of the Palais du Luxembourg (now the Senate) are terraces, paths and a wide tree-lined alley that leads down to the Observatory crossroads. Natural attractions include shady chestnut trees, potted orange- and palm-trees, lawns and even an experimental fruit-garden and orchard, while fountains, tennis-courts, bee hives, a puppet-theatre and children's playgrounds offer other distractions. Statues of the queens of France, artists and writers are dotted about the terraces and avenues.

Park activities All year round joggers work off their *foie gras* on the circumference, and in summer sunbathers and bookworms settle into park chairs, card- and chess-playing retirees claim the shade in front of the palace, bands tune up at the bandstand near the Boulevard Saint-Michel entrance, and children burn off energy on swings and donkeys.

History The Palais du Luxembourg and surrounding garden were originally commissioned by Marie de Médicis, wife of Henri IV, in 1615, and designed to resemble her Florentine childhood home. The Allée de l'Observatoire and the English-style garden were added in the early 19th century. A petition signed by 12,000 Parisians luckily saved the garden from Haussmann's urban ambitions, and since then its formal charms have inspired countless literary and celluloid tributes.

HIGHLIGHTS

- Médicis fountain
- Cyclops, Acis and Galateus sculptures
- Bandstand
- Statue of Delacroix
- Orange-tree conservatory
- Experimental fruit-garden
- Bee-keeping school
- Statues of queens of France

DID YOU KNOW?

- Isadora Duncan danced here
- Ernest Hemingway claimed to capture pigeons here for his supper

INFORMATION

- G7
- 15 rue de Vaugirard 75006
- Senate: 01 42 34 20 00
- Apr–Oct daily 7:30AM–9:30PM. Nov–Mar daily 8.15–5 (times may vary slightly)
- Open-air cafés; kiosk restaurant
- Luxembourg
- 21, 27, 38, 58, 82, 84, 85, 89
- RER Line B Luxembourg
- Very good
- Free
- Eglise de Saint-Sulpice (► 52)

15

MUSÉE DE CLUNY

INFORMATION

- H7
- 6 Place Paul-Painlevé 75006
- 01 53 73 78 00
- Wed–Mon 9:15–5:45
- Cluny-La Sorbonne
- 21, 27, 38, 63, 85, 86, 87, 96
- Moderate
- Sainte-Chapelle (► 39)
- Guided tours of vaults: Wed, Sat, Sun 2PM. Tours of collection at 3:30PM

Top: A mon Seul Désir, *one of the* La Dame à la Licorne *tapestries*

"*Take a deep breath outside the Musée de Cluny (officially the Musée National du Moyen-Age/Thermes de Cluny) and prepare to enter a time-warp, in which the days of the troubadours and courtly love are re-created in its panelled rooms.***"**

Baths The late 2nd-century Gallo-Roman baths adjoining the Hôtel de Cluny are composed of three stone chambers: the Caldarium (steam bath), the Tepidarium (tepid bath) and the Frigidarium (cold bath), with ruins of the former gymnasium visible on the Boulevard Saint-Germain side. Important Roman stonework is exhibited in the niches, while Room VIII houses 21 mutilated heads from Notre-Dame. Recent excavations have also opened up a labyrinth of Roman vaults which can be toured with a guide.

Treasures The Gothic turreted mansion was built in 1500 by the abbot Jacques d'Amboise and is one of France's finest examples of domestic architecture of this period. Some 23,000 objects compose the collection, much of which was gathered by the 19th-century medievalist and collector, Alexandre du Sommerard. Perhaps the most famous piece is the beautiful *La Dame à la Licorne* tapestry, woven in the late 15th century. Six enigmatic panels depict a woman, a lion and a unicorn, animals, flowers and birds, all exquisitely worked. Costumes, accessories, textiles and tapestries are of Byzantine, Coptic or European origin, while the gold- and metalwork room houses some outstanding pieces of Gallic, Barbarian, Merovingian and Visigoth artistry. Stained glass, table-games, ceramics, woodcarvings, illuminated manuscripts and Books of Hours, altarpieces and religious statuary complete this exceptional and very manageable display.

SAINTE-CHAPELLE

"Sainte-Chapelle's 75m spire soaring towards the heavens is in itself an extra-ordinary expression of faith, but inside this is surpassed by the glowing intensity of the magnificent stained-glass windows reaching up to a star-studded roof."

Masterpiece One of Paris's oldest and most significant monuments stands within the precincts of the Palais de Justice. The chapel was built by Louis IX (later canonised) to house relics he had acquired at exorbitant cost during the crusades, and which included what was reputed to be the Crown of Thorns, as well as fragments of the

Cross and drops of Christ's blood (now kept in Notre-Dame). Pierre de Montreuil master-minded this delicate Gothic construction, bypassing the use of flying buttresses, incorporating a lower chapel for palace servants and instal-ling 618sq m of stained glass above. Completed in 1248 in record time, it served as Louis IX's private chapel with discreet access from what was then the royal palace.

Apocalypse No fewer than 1,134 biblical scenes are illustrated in the 16 windows, starting with Genesis and finishing with the Apocalypse (the central rose window). To follow the narrative chronologically, read from left to right and bottom to top, row by row. The statues of Apostles against the pillars are mostly copies – the damaged originals are at the Musée de Cluny.

HIGHLIGHTS

- Rose window
- Oratory
- 19th-century restoration
- Tombs of canons
- Stained-glass depiction of Christ's Passion
- St Louis himself in the 15th window

INFORMATION

- ✚ H6
- ✉ 4 Boulevard du Palais 75001
- ☎ 01 53 73 78 51
- 🕐 Oct–Mar daily 10–4:30. Apr–Sep daily 9:30–6
- Ⓜ Cité, Saint-Michel
- 🚌 21, 38, 85, 96
- Ⓡ RER Line B, Saint-Michel
- ♿ Moderate
- ↔ Musée de Cluny (➤ 38)

Top: the stained-glass windows of the upper chapel

17

CONCIERGERIE

HIGHLIGHTS

- Public clock
- Sculptures
- Barber's cell
- Tour Bonbec

DID YOU KNOW?

- 288 prisoners were massacred here in 1792
- 4,164 citizens were held here during the Terror
- Comte d'Armagnac was assassinated here
- 22 left-wing Girondins were held in one room
- Robespierre spent only one night here before his execution
- There were three types of cell according to prisoners' means

INFORMATION

- H6
- 1 Quai de l'Horloge 75001
- 01 53 73 78 50
- Oct–Mar daily 10–4:30. Apr–Sep daily 9:30–6
- Cité, Châtelet
- 21, 38, 85, 96
- Moderate
- Sainte-Chapelle (➤ 39)
- Guided tours: daily 11AM, 3PM

" *The ghosts of the victims of the guillotine must surely haunt this stark and gloomy place, which served as a prison and torture chamber for over five centuries, and which remains full of macabre mementoes of its grisly past.* **"**

Gloom Rising over the Seine in menacing splendour, the turreted Conciergerie was built in 1299–1313 originally to house Philippe-le-Bel's caretaker (*concierge*) and palace guards, and with Sainte-Chapelle it formed part of a royal complex on the Ile de la Cité. The square corner tower displays Paris's first public clock, an ornate masterpiece constructed in 1370 and restored along with the rest of the Gothic interior in the 19th century. Access to the Conciergerie is through the Salle des Gardes, a vaulted stone chamber now plunged into shadow by the embankment outside, which in turn opens on to the vast but equally gloomy Salle des Gens d'Armes. This is thought to be Europe's oldest-surviving medieval hall, and it is where members of the royal household ate their meals. From here, a curious spiral staircase leads to the original kitchens.

Victims From 1391 until 1914 the building functioned as a prison and torture chamber, its reputation striking terror into the hearts of thousands. A network of cells, both shared and private, lines the corridor (the rue de Paris) leading to the Galerie des Prisonniers, where lawyers, prisoners and visitors once mingled. A staircase leads up to rooms relating the Conciergerie's bloody history (including a list of the guillotine's 2,278 victims); back downstairs are re-creations of the Chapelle des Girondins, and the cells occupied by Marie-Antoinette, Danton and Robespierre.

Top: Salle des Gens d'Armes

CENTRE GEORGES POMPIDOU

"Late opening hours make an exhibition visit possible between an aperitif and dinner in this still-controversial cultural centre. You can take your pick between the genesis of modernism, an art film, or a drama performance."

High-tech culture More than a mere landmark in the extensive face-lift that Paris has undergone in the last 20 years, the high-tech Centre Pompidou (commonly known as Beaubourg) is a hive of constantly changing cultural activity. Contemporary art, architecture, design, photography, theatre, cinema and dance are all represented, while the lofty structure itself offers exceptional views over central Paris. Take the transparent escalator tubes for a bird's-eye view of the piazza below, where musicians, street artists and portraitists ply their trades to the teeming crowds.

The fountain in nearby Place Igor Stravinsky

Face-lift From October 1997 to the eve of the millennium in December 1999, the centre will undergo major restructuring and refurbishing. Radically reduced exhibition space and access to the top-floor panoramas remain, but otherwise the centre is essentially closed. On reopening in the year 2000, the layout will have gained in logic but lost in atmosphere. In the meantime, visit the reopened Atelier Brancusi on the piazza or spend francs at the museum shop housed in the temporary tepee in front of the centre.

HIGHLIGHTS

- Design by Richard Rogers, Renzo Piano and Gianfranco Franchini
- Stravinsky fountain
- *The Deep*, Jackson Pollock
- *Phoque*, Brancusi
- *Le Magasin*, Ben
- *Bleu II*, Miró
- *Infiltration homogène*, Joseph Beuys
- Gouache cut-outs, Matisse
- *Improvisations*, Kandinsky
- Electronic countdown to the year 2000

INFORMATION

- 🖽 H5/6
- ✉ Rue Rambuteau 75004
- ☎ 01 44 78 12 33.
  Information on daily events: 01 42 77 11 12
- 🕙 Mon, Wed–Fri noon–10PM. Sat–Sun 10–10
- 🍴 Mediocre cafeteria with a view
- Ⓜ Rambuteau, Hôtel de Ville
- 🚌 38, 47
- Ⓡ RER Line A B, Châtelet-Les Halles
- ♿ Excellent
- 💷 Very expensive; free on Sun 10–2
- ↔ Musée National des Techniques (▶ 51)
- ❓ Guided and audio tours to Musée National d'Art Moderne; frequent lectures, concerts, parallel activities, Atelier des Enfants

19

MARCHÉ AUX PUCES DE SAINT-OUEN

INFORMATION

- ✚ G1
- ✉ Porte de Clignancourt
- ⏰ Sat–Mon 7:30–5
- 🍴 Cafés and restaurants on rue des Rosiers
- 🚇 Porte de Clignancourt, Porte de Saint-Ouen
- 🚌 56, 60, 81, 95
- ♿ Good
- 💷 Free
- ↔ Sacré-Coeur (➤ 33)
- ❓ Beware of pickpockets

"My classic Sunday occupations cannot be called original as they often revolve around the Paris flea markets, of which the crème de la crème *is still this one. Nowhere else can you find such a fascinating cross-section of Parisian society."*

Duck and banter The approach from the métro to this sprawling 30-ha market is hardly inspiring as it entails bypassing household goods, jeans and shoe-stands before ducking under the *périphérique* flyover and finally entering the fray. Persevere and you may discover an antique gem, a fake, or a second-hand pilot's jacket. Everything and anything is displayed here but all commerce is carried on in the true bantering style of the *faubourgs*, a habit which dates from the late 19th century when the first rag-and-bone men moved in to offer their wares for sale.

Bargain Registered dealers are divided into seven official markets which interconnect through passageways bustling with crowds. Along the fringes are countless hopefuls who set up temporary stands to sell a mind-boggling range of goods from obsolete kitchenware to old juke boxes and cheap junk. Although unashamedly a tourist trap, there is something for everyone here, but do go early – trading starts at 7:30AM. Bargaining is obligatory and prices are directly related to the weather: high on sunny, crowded days and low under cold, wet skies. Stop for lunch in one of the animated bistros along the rue des Rosiers – try the garden setting of Chez la Mère Marie at No 82 (☎ 01 40 11 90 48). At weekends as many as 150,000 bargain-hunters, tourists and dealers can cram the passageways – avoid Sunday afternoons in particular, when the throng reaches claustrophobic proportions and pickpockets abound.

NOTRE-DAME

❝ *'Spectacular' is the word that springs to mind when describing Paris's most extraordinary monument, with its 90m spire and some of the world's best-known flying buttresses. One of my favourite views of it is from the* quais *to the east.* ❞

Evolution Construction started on this labour of love and faith in 1163 but it was not finished until 1345, so making it transitional in style between Romanesque and Gothic. Since then the cathedral has suffered from pollution, politics, aesthetic trends and religious change. Louis XV declared stained glass outmoded and replaced most of the rose windows with clear glass (the stained glass was later restored), Revolutionary anti-clericalism toppled countless statues and the spire was amputated in 1787. Not least, Viollet-le-Duc, the fervent 19th-century medievalist architect, was let loose on its restoration and made radical alterations.

Interior grandeur The gloomy stone interior contains numerous chapels, tombs and statues, as well as the sacristy (south side of choir) where the treasure of Notre-Dame is kept. Climb the towers (386 steps) for fantastic views and a close-up on the gargoyles. Look closely at the three asymmetrical sculpted portals on the cathedral's façade: these once served as a Bible for illiterate worshippers. Finally, walk around the cathedral for a view of its extravagant flying buttresses.

HIGHLIGHTS

- South rose window
- Porte Rouge
- Portail du Cloître
- Sculptures of Ste Anne
- Treasure of Notre-Dame
- Emmanuel bell
- 1730 organ
- *Pietà*, Nicolas Coustou
- Statue of Notre-Dame de Paris
- Choir stalls

INFORMATION

- ✚ H6
- ✉ Place du Parvis Notre-Dame 75004
- ☎ 01 42 34 56 10; crypt, 01 43 29 83 51
- ◷ Cathedral: daily 8–7. Tower and crypt: Oct–Mar daily 10–4:30. Apr–Sep daily 10–5:30
- 🚇 Cité, Saint-Michel
- 🚌 24, 47
- 🚇 RER Lines B and C, Saint-Michel
- ♿ Good
- 💰 Cathedral: free. Tower and crypt: moderate
- ↔ Musée de Cluny (➤ 38), Ile Saint-Louis (➤ 44)
- ❓ Organ recitals at 5:30PM on Sun

The southern aspect of Notre-Dame, showing the south rose window (detail above)

43

21

ILE SAINT-LOUIS

"Floating mid-Seine is this fascinating residential island, a living museum of 17th-century architecture and also a popular tourist haunt. Join the crowds and spot an illustrious resident, but above all indulge in the island's own ice-cream."

History Once a marshy swamp, the Ile Saint-Louis was transformed into an elegant residential area in the 17th century, when it was joined to the

Ile de la Cité. Today, six bridges link it to the Rive Droite and the Rive Gauche, but nevertheless it still maintains a spirit of its own, and local residents brazenly declare that its food shops are unsurpassable. Cutting across it lengthwise is rue Saint-Louis-en-l'Ile,

Courtyard, Quai de Bourbon

lined with up-market groceries, arts and craft shops and restaurants, and home to the Eglise Saint-Louis-en-l'Isle begun by Le Vau in 1664. The side-streets here are mainly residential.

Hashish The Quai d'Anjou, on the north-eastern side, has a rich past. Former residents include the architect himself, Le Vau, at No 3, Honoré Daumier (No 9), Baudelaire, and Théophile Gautier who, at No 17, animated his Club des Haschichins. Commemorative plaques to the famous pepper the façades of the island's harmonious townhouses, and the riverside paths offer quintessential Parisian views, romantic trysts and summer sunbathing. Before leaving, make sure you try a Berthillon ice-cream, reputedly the best in the world!

INSTITUT DU MONDE ARABE

"It is difficult to miss this gleaming, ultra-contemporary building as you cross the Seine. Although I find it limited, the museum's collection nevertheless offers a sleekly presented introduction to the brilliance of Islamic civilisation."

Arab inspiration Clean lines, aluminium walls and glass are the hallmarks of Jean Nouvel's design for the Arab Institute, which was inaugurated in 1980 to foster cultural exchange between Islamic countries and the West. Innovative features include high-speed transparent lifts, a system of high-tech metal screens on the south elevation which filter light entering the institute and which were inspired by the *musharabia* (carved wooden screens) on traditional Arab buildings, and an enclosed courtyard achieved by splitting the building in two. The institute's facilities comprise a museum, library, exhibition halls, lecture and concert halls, and an elegant roof-top café boasting spectacular panoramas across the Seine.

Museum First take the lift to the 9th floor for sweeping views across the Ile Saint-Louis and north-eastern Paris, then head down to the museum on the 7th floor. Here, finely crafted metalwork, ceramics, textiles, carpets and calligraphy reflect the exceptional talents of Islamic civilisation, although the collection remains small in relation to its ambitious setting. Temporary exhibitions are often of a high quality and cover both historical and contemporary themes in art, crafts or photography. There is an audio-visual centre in the basement with thousands of slides, photographs, films and sound recordings, and current news broadcasts from all over the Arab world are also available for viewing.

HIGHLIGHTS

- Light screens
- Astrolabes in museum
- Statue of Amma'alay
- Head of sun god
- Rope and palm-fibre sandal
- Sultan Selim III's Koran
- Miniature of Emperor Aurengzeb
- Indian glass vase
- Egyptian child's tunic

INFORMATION

- J7
- 1 rue des Fossés Saint-Bernard 75005
- 01 40 51 38 38
- Tue–Sun 10–6
- Convivial snack bar open until midnight; tea-room
- Jussieu, Cardinal Lemoine
- 24, 63, 67, 86, 87, 89
- Excellent
- Moderate
- Ile Saint-Louis (➤ 44), Arènes de Lutèce (➤ 59)
- Occasional Arab music, films and plays

45

MUSÉE CARNAVALET

INFORMATION

"There is no better museum than this to plunge you into the history of Paris, and its renovated mansion setting is hard to beat. Period rooms, artefacts, documents, paintings and objets d'art combine to swing you through the city's turbulent past."

Ornamental excess This captivating collection is displayed within two adjoining 16th- and 17th-century townhouses. Entrance is through the superb courtyard of the Hôtel Carnavalet (1548), once home to the celebrated writer Madame de Sévigné. Here attention focuses on the Roman period, the Middle Ages, the Renaissance, and the heights of decorative excess reached under Louis XIV, Louis XV and Louis XVI. Some of the richly painted and sculpted interiors are original to the building, others, such as the wood-panelling from the Hôtel Colbert de Villacerf and Brunetti's *trompe-l'oeil* staircase paintings, have been brought in.

Revolution to the present Next door, the smartly renovated Hôtel Le Peletier de Saint-Fargeau (1690) exhibits some remarkable objects from the Revolution – a period when anything and everything was emblazoned with slogans – and continues with Napoleon I's reign, the Restoration, the Second Empire, the Commune and finally the Belle Epoque. Illustrious figures such as Robespierre and Madame Le Récamier come to life within their chronological context. The collection ends in the early 20th century with some remarkable reconstructions of interiors, and paintings by Utrillo, Signac, Marquet and Foujita.

PLACE DES VOSGES

"Paris's best-preserved square connects the quarters of the Marais and the Bastille. I always marvel at its architectural unity and love to stroll under its arcades, now animated by outdoor restaurants and window-shoppers."

Place Royale Ever since the square was inaugurated in 1612 with a spectacular fireworks display, countless luminaries have chosen to live in the red-brick houses overlooking the central garden of plane trees. Before that, the square was the site of a royal palace, the Palais des Tournelles (1407), which was later abandoned and demolished by Catherine de Médicis in 1559 when her husband Henri II died in a tournament. The arcaded façades were commissioned by the enlightened Henri IV, who incorporated two royal pavilions at the centre of the north and south sides of the square and named it 'Place Royale'.

Celebrities After the Revolution the square was renamed Place des Vosges in honour of the first French district to pay its new taxes. The first example of planned development in the history of Paris, these 36 townhouses (nine on each side and still intact after four centuries) with their steep-pitched roofs surround a formal garden laid out with gravel paths and fountains. The elegant symmetry of the houses has always attracted a string of celebrities. Princesses, official mistresses, Cardinal Richelieu, the Duc de Sully, Victor Hugo (his house is now a museum) and Théophile Gautier, and more recently the late painter Francis Bacon, Beaubourg's architect Richard Rogers and former minister of culture, Jack Lang, have all lived here. Up-market shops and chic art galleries, with prices to match and perfect for window-gazing, line its arcades.

HIGHLIGHTS

- Pavillon du Roi
- Statue of Louis XIII
- Hôtel de Coulanges
- No 6, Maison Victor Hugo
- No 21, residence of Cardinal Richelieu
- Archaeological finds at No 18
- Door-knockers
- *Trompe-l'oeil* bricks
- Auvergne sausages at Ma Bourgogne restaurant

INFORMATION

- ✚ J6
- ✉ Place des Vosges 75004
- 🍽 Ma Bourgogne (► 73)
- 🚇 Bastille, Chemin-Vert, Saint Paul
- 🚌 29, 96
- ♿ Good
- 🎫 Free
- ↔ Hôtel de Sully (► 17), Musée Carnavalet (► 46)

25

CIMETIÈRE DU PÈRE LACHAISE

- Oscar Wilde's tomb
- Edith Piaf's tomb
- Chopin's tomb
- Marcel Proust's tomb
- Mur des Fédérés
- Delacroix's tomb
- Tomb of Victor Hugo's family
- Baron Haussmann's tomb
- Molière's tomb
- Jim Morrison's tomb

INFORMATION

- ✚ L/M5/6
- ✉ Boulevard de Ménilmontant 75020
- ☎ 01 43 70 70 33
- 🕐 Oct–Mar daily 8–5:30. Apr–Sep Mon–Fri 8–6; Sat 8:30–5:30/6; Sun 9–5:30/6
- 🚇 Père Lachaise
- 🚌 61, 69
- ♿ Excellent
- ✋ Free

"*If you think cemeteries are lugubrious, then I recommend a visit to Père Lachaise to change your mind. A plethora of tomb designs, shady trees and twisting paths combine to create a peaceful setting that has become a popular park.***"**

Pilgrimage This landscaped hillside, up in the *faubourgs* of Ménilmontant, is now a favourite haunt for rock fans, Piaf fans, and lovers of poetry, literature, music and history. Since its creation in 1803 this vast cemetery has seen hundreds of the famous and illustrious buried or cremated within its precincts, so that a walk around its labyrinthine expanse presents a microcosm of French socio-cultural history. Pick up a plan at the entrance or the kiosk by the métro, then set off on this Parisian path of the Holy Grail to track down your heroes.

Incumbents The cemetery was created in 1803 on land once owned by Louis XIV's confessor, Father La Chaise. It was the site of the Communards' tragic last stand in 1871, when the 147 survivors of a night-long fight met their bloody end in front of a government firing-squad and were thrown into a communal grave, now commemorated by the Mur des Fédérés in the eastern corner. A sombre reminder of the victims of World War II are the memorials to those who died in the Nazi concentration camps. Paths meander past striking funerary monuments and the graves of such well-known figures as the star-crossed medieval lovers Abélard and Héloïse, painters Delacroix and Modigliani, actress Sarah Bernhardt, composers Poulenc and Bizet, and writers Balzac and Colette. Crowds of rock fans throng around the tomb of Jim Morrison, singer with The Doors, whose death in Paris in 1971 is still a mystery.

PARIS's
best

MUSEUMS & GALLERIES

Other museums

If you are hooked on the intimate atmosphere of one-man museums, then head for the former home-studio of sculptor Antoine Bourdelle, recently renovated by top architect Christian de Portzamparc (✉ 18 rue Antoine Bourdelle 75014 🚇 Falguière). Other jewels include the Maison Victor Hugo (➤ 47), the Musée Delacroix (➤ 60), the Musée Hébert (➤ 60), and the Maison de Balzac (47 rue Raynouard 75016 🚇 Passy).

Visit the Musée d'Art Moderne for modern and contemporary paintings and sculpture

CITÉ DES SCIENCES ET DE L'INDUSTRIE

A vast, enthralling display covering the earth, the universe, life, communications, natural resources, technology and industry. There are temporary exhibitions, a planetarium, a children's section and a THX cinema, La Géode (➤ 58).

➕ L2 ✉ 30 Avenue Corentin Cariou 75019 ☎ 08 36 68 29 30 🕒 Tue–Sat 10–6; Sun 10–7 🍽 Cafés in park 🚇 Porte de la Villette 💶 Very expensive

MAISON EUROPÉENNE DE LA PHOTOGRAPHIE

A stylish new centre for contemporary photography, which has permanent displays and stages dynamic temporary shows.

➕ J6 ✉ 5–7 rue du Fourcy 75004 ☎ 01 44 78 75 00 🕒 Wed–Sat 11AM–8PM 🚇 Saint-Paul 💶 Moderate

MUSÉE D'ART MODERNE DE LA VILLE DE PARIS

Dufy's mural *La Fée Electricité*, Matisse's *La Danse* and a solid collection of the early moderns offer a parallel to exhibitions of the contemporary avant-garde.

➕ D5 ✉ 11 Avenue du Président Wilson 75016 ☎ 01 53 67 40 00 🕒 Tue, Thu–Fri 10–5:30; Wed 10–8:30; Sat–Sun 10–7 🍽 Cafeteria 🚇 Iéna, Alma-Marceau 💶 Expensive

MUSÉE GUSTAVE MOREAU

This museum is dedicated solely to the Symbolist painter Gustave Moreau (teacher of Matisse and Rouault), and is housed in his former home-studio.

Atmospheric paintings, watercolours and drawings.

🔲 G4 ✉ 14 rue de la Rochefoucauld 75009 ☎ 01 48 74 38 50 🕐 Thu–Sun 10–12:45, 2–5:15; Mon and Wed 11–5:15 🚇 Trinité 💵 Moderate

MUSÉE NATIONAL DES ARTS AFRICAINS ET OCÉANIENS

Fascinating artefacts from the Pacific, Africa and Maghreb, extending to Australian aboriginal art. Sculptures, textiles, jewellery and masks. Kids love the aquariums, and the building (1931) is stunning.

🔲 M8 ✉ 293 Avenue Daumesnil 75012 ☎ 01 44 74 84 80; 01 43 46 51 61 🕐 Wed–Mon 10–12, 1:30–5:30; Sat–Sun 12:30–6 🚇 Porte Dorée 💵 Moderate

MUSÉE NATIONAL DES TECHNIQUES

An eccentric museum where art meets science through antique clocks, glass, vintage cars, optics and mechanical toys. Undergoing massive renovation; some parts remain closed until 1998.

🔲 J5 ✉ 292 rue Saint-Martin 75003 ☎ 01 40 27 23 31 🕐 Tue–Sun 10–5 🚇 Arts et Métiers, Réaumur-Sébastopol 💵 Moderate

MUSÉE DU PANTHÉON BOUDDHIQUE (GUIMET)

While the magnificent Musée Guimet remains closed for major restructuring until mid-1999, visit the annexe to meditate on Japanese and Chinese Buddhas.

🔲 D5 ✉ 19 Avenue d'Iéna 75116 ☎ 01 47 23 61 65 🚇 Wed–Mon 9:45–5:45 🚇 Iéna 💵 Moderate

MUSÉE PICASSO

A massive collection of Picasso's paintings, sculptures, drawings and ceramics in a beautifully renovated 17th-century mansion. The fixtures are by Diego Giacometti and some of the works are by Picasso's contemporaries.

🔲 J6 ✉ Hôtel Salé, 5 rue de Thorigny 75003 ☎ 01 42 71 25 21 🕐 Wed–Mon 9:30–5:30 🚇 Chemin Vert 🚌 29 💵 Moderate

MUSÉUM NATIONAL D'HISTOIRE NATURELLE

Spectacular displays of comparative anatomy, paleontology and mineralogy. Interesting temporary exhibitions and botanic gardens (1635).

🔲 J8 ✉ 57 rue Cuvier 75005 ☎ 01 40 79 30 00 🕐 Wed–Mon 10–5; Thu 10–10. Entomology: 1–5 🚇 Monge, Gare d'Austeritz 💵 Expensive; reduced in morning

Grand Nu au Fauteuil Rouge *(1929), in the Picasso Museum*

Musée Picasso

The contents of the Musée Picasso – no fewer than 200 paintings, 158 sculptures and 3,000 drawings – were acquired by France in lieu of death duties. The process of evaluating Picasso's vast estate was no simple task as he had the annoying habit of moving château once the rooms were filled with his prodigious works. Eleven years of cataloguing followed by legal wrangling with his heirs finally produced this superb selection, one-quarter of his collection.

51

PLACES OF WORSHIP

Saint-Etienne-du-Mont

Saint-Germain-des-Prés

The first church of Saint-Germain-des-Prés was erected in the 6th century in the middle of fields (*les prés*). From the 8th century the abbey was part of a Benedictine monastery but was destroyed by the Normans, after which the present church was built. The abbey was surrounded by a fortified wall and adjoined a bishop's palace, but this eventually made way for housing in the late 17th century.

EGLISE SAINT-ETIENNE-DU-MONT
Bizarre architectural combination of Gothic, Renaissance and classical dating from the 15th century. Unique carved rood screen over the nave.
H7 ⊠ Place Sainte-Genevieve 75005 🚇 Cardinal Lemoine

EGLISE DE SAINT-EUSTACHE
Renaissance in detail and decoration but medieval in general design. Frequent organ recitals.
H5 ⊠ Rue Rambuteau 75001 🚇 Les Halles

EGLISE DE SAINT-GERMAIN-DES-PRÉS
Paris's oldest abbey dates from the 10th century; it preserves 12th-century flying buttresses, an original tower and a choir. Regular organ recitals.
G6 ⊠ Place Saint-Germain-des-Prés 75006
🚇 Saint-Germain-des-Prés

EGLISE DE SAINT-MERRI
Superb example of Flamboyant Gothic though not completed until 1612. Renaissance stained glass, murals, an impressive organ loft and Paris's oldest bell (1331). Concerts are held regularly.
H6 ⊠ 78 rue Saint-Martin 75003 🚇 Hôtel de Ville

EGLISE DE SAINT-SÉVERIN
Rebuilt in the 13th–16th centuries the on site of a 12th-century oratory. Inside is an impressive double ambulatory, palm-tree vaulting and the Chapelle Mansart. Some stained glass originated at Saint-Germain-des-Prés (late 14th century).
H6 ⊠ 1 rue des Prêtres Saint-Séverin 75005 🚇 Saint-Michel

EGLISE DE SAINT-SULPICE
Construction started in 1646 and ended 134 years later, producing asymmetrical towers and very mixed styles. Note Delacroix's murals in the first chapel on the right, France's largest organ and statues by Bouchardon.
G7 ⊠ Place Saint-Sulpice 75006 🕐 7:30–7:30
🚇 Saint-Sulpice

LA MOSQUÉE
This startling Moorish construction (1926) has a richly decorated interior, patio and arcaded garden. Relax in the hammam (see panel ➤ 85) or sip mint tea.
J8 ⊠ Place du Puits-de-l'Ermite 75005 ☎ 01 45 35 97 33
🕐 Guided tours: 9–12, 2–6. Closed Fri 🍴 Tea-room 🚇 Monge
💲 Cheap

CULT CAFÉS

LES DEUX MAGOTS

Some 25 whisky brands, a good concentration of tourists, and the literary shades of Mallarmé, André Breton and Hemingway. Strategic spot for street-artists.

🔟 G6 ✉ 6 Place Saint-Germain-des-Prés 75006 ☎ 01 45 48 55 25 🕐 Daily 7:30AM–2AM 🚇 Saint-Germain-des-Prés

Les Deux Magots, in Place Saint-Germain-des-Prés

CAFÉ BEAUBOURG

Opposite Beaubourg, and a favourite with artists, critics and book-eating poseurs. Discreet tables in spacious setting designed by Christian de Portzamparc. A good winter retreat.

🔟 H6 ✉ 100 rue Saint-Martin 75004 ☎ 01 48 87 89 98 🕐 Daily 8AM–2AM 🚇 Hôtel de Ville

LA CLOSERIE DES LILAS

Hot spot of history's makers and shakers, including Lenin, Trotsky, Verlaine and James Joyce.

🔟 G8 ✉ 171 Boulevard du Montparnasse 75006 ☎ 01 43 26 70 50 🕐 Daily 11AM–1:30AM 🚇 Vavin, Raspail

CAFÉ DE FLORE

Haunted by ghosts of existentialists Sartre and De Beauvoir, who held court here during the Occupation. Wildly overpriced but great for people-watching.

🔟 G6 ✉ 172 Boulevard Saint-Germain ☎ 01 45 48 55 26 🕐 Daily 7:45AM–1:30AM 🚇 Saint-Germain-des-Prés

CAFÉ MARLY

The latest in fashionable watering-holes. Elegance is assured by the setting overlooking the Louvre pyramid, and by Olivier Gagnère's intelligent decoration.

🔟 G5 ✉ Cour Napoléon, 93 rue de Rivoli 75001 ☎ 01 49 26 06 60 🕐 Daily 8AM–2AM 🚇 Palais-Royal/Musée du Louvre

CAFÉ DE LA PAIX

Excessively mid-19th century décor designed by Charles Garnier. Over-the-top setting. Touristy.

🔟 G4 ✉ 12 Boulevard des Capucines 75009 ☎ 01 40 07 30 20 🕐 Daily 10AM–1AM 🚇 Opéra

LA PALETTE

Firmly established Left Bank arty bar/café. Run with an iron glove by bearded Jean-François, not to be trifled with. Lovely tree-shaded terrace in summer.

🔟 G6 ✉ 43 rue de Seine 75006 ☎ 01 43 26 84 87 🕐 Mon–Sat 8AM–2AM. Closed Aug 🚇 Odéon.

The croissant

As you sit over your morning *café au lait* chewing a croissant, meditate on the origins of this quintessential French product. It was invented when Vienna was besieged by the Turks in 1683. A baker heard underground noises and informed the authorities, who found the enemy tunnelling away into the city. The baker's reward was permission to produce pastries – so he created one in the form of the Islamic crescent.

53

20TH-CENTURY ARCHITECTURE

See Top 25 Sights for
CENTRE GEORGES POMPIDOU ➤ 41
INSTITUT DU MONDE ARABE ➤ 45

Grands projets

President Mitterrand is responsible for many of Paris's late 20th-century monuments. For over a decade cranes groaned as the state's *grands projets* emerged from their foundations. Intellectual criteria often came before functional considerations, and consequently not all monuments operate successfully. The Louvre renovation, topped by I M Pei's pyramid, is a notable exception.

BIBLIOTHÈQUE DE FRANCE

Mitterrand's last pet *grand projet*. Dominique Perrault's symbolic design was dogged by technical and functional problems until it finally opened in early 1997.

➕ K8　✉ 9 Boulevard Vincent Auriol 75013　☎ 01 53 79 53 79　◉ Open to researchers only　🚇 Quai de la Gare

CITÉ DE LA MUSIQUE

Finally completed in 1995 after 16 years of procrastination and political volte-faces. Monumental design in white stone by Christian de Portzamparc houses a music school, concert hall and museum of music.

➕ L2　✉ Parc de la Villette　☎ 01 44 84 45 45　◉ Tue–Sun noon–6　🍴 Café　🚇 Porte de Pantin

LA GRANDE ARCHE

A marble window on the world designed by Otto Von Spreckelsen and completed for the 1989 Bicentenary. Take the vertiginous outside lift to the top for views along Le Nôtre's historical axis to the Louvre.

➕ Off map at A2　✉ 1 Parvis de La Défense　☎ 01 49 07 27 57　◉ Oct–Mar Mon–Fri 10–6. Apr–Sep Mon–Fri 10–7; Sat–Sun 9–8　🚇 La Défense　💲 Expensive

MAISON DU VERRE

Designed in art deco style by Pierre Chareau in 1932. Astonishing use of glass.

➕ G6　✉ 31 rue Saint-Guillaume 75006　🚇 Rue du Bac

NO 26 RUE VAVIN

Innovative building faced in blue and white ceramic with stepped balconies. Designed by Henri Sauvage in 1925 as an early attempt at a self-contained unit.

➕ G7　✉ 26 rue Vavin 75006　🚇 Vavin

PORTE DAUPHINE

The best remaining example (1902) of Hector Guimard's art nouveau métro entrances, with a glass canopy and writhing sculptural structures.

➕ C4　✉ Avenue Bugeaud 75016　🚇 Porte Dauphine

RUE MALLET-STEVENS

This tiny cul-de-sac houses major symbols of 'cubist' architecture (1927) by Robert Mallet-Stevens. The stark, purist lines and volumes continue at Le Corbusier's nearby Villa La Roche (1923), now a foundation.

➕ B6　✉ Rue Mallet-Stevens, off rue du Dr Blanche 75016　🚇 Jasmin

The Grande Arche at La Défense

BRIDGES

PONT ALEXANDRE III
Paris's most ornate bridge, rich in gilded cupids and elaborate lamps. Built for the 1900 Exposition Universelle and dedicated to the new Franco-Russian alliance – the foundation stone was laid by Tsar Alexander III.
➕ E5 🚇 Invalides

PONT DE L'ALMA
Originally built in 1856 to commemorate victory over the Russians in the Crimean War. Replaced in 1974 but the Zouave soldier remains, one of four original statues, now acting as a high-water marker.
➕ E5 🚇 Alma-Marceau

PONT DES ARTS
The pedestrian bridge of 1804 was replaced in 1985 by an iron structure of seven steel arches crossed by resonant wooden planks. A favourite spot for impromptu parties, buskers and commercial artists.
➕ G6 🚇 Louvre-Rivoli

PONT DE BIR-HAKEIM
Paris's double-decker bridge, best experienced by rattling over it in a métro. Built 1903–5 with metal columns in art nouveau style designed by Formigé.
➕ D6 🚇 Bir-Hakeim, Passy

PONT MARIE
Named after the Ile Saint-Louis property developer, and built in 1635. Once lined with four-storey houses – some later partly destroyed by floods and others demolished in 1788.
➕ J6 🚇 Pont Marie

PONT NEUF
Built 1578–1604, Paris's oldest bridge ironically bears the name of 'New Bridge'. The innovative, houseless design was highly controversial at the time. In 1985 it was 'wrapped' by land-artist Christo.
➕ G/H6 🚇 Pont Neuf

PONT ROYAL
Five classical arches join the Tuileries with the Faubourg Saint-Germain area. Built in 1689 by Gabriel to Mansart's design, the bridge was once used for major Parisian festivities and fireworks.
➕ G6 🚇 Palais-Royal/Musée du Louvre

36 bridges
The Paris motto '*Fluctuat nec mergitur*' ('It floats but it never sinks') did not always hold true for its bridges. For centuries there were only two, linking the Ile de la Cité north and south. Subsequent wooden bridges sank without trace after floods, fires or rivercraft collisions, so the construction of the stone Pont Neuf marked a real advance. The city's 36th bridge, Pont Charles de Gaulle, now spans the Seine between the Bibliothèque de France and Bercy.

Pont Alexandre III

GREEN SPACES

Parc Monceau

Parc de Bagatelle

On the west side of the Bois de Boulogne is the Parc de Bagatelle. Its mini-château, built in 1775, was sold in 1870 to Englishman Richard Wallace, who added further pavilions and terraces. About 700 varieties of roses bloom here and its open-air restaurant offers a romantic summer-evening setting (see panel ➤ 66).

Jardin des Serres d'Auteuil

Off the tourist beat and with striking late-19th century tropical greenhouses. The terrace wall is adorned with sculpted masks from Rodin's studio (➕ A7 ✉ 3 Avenue de la Porte d'Auteuil *3216* ☎ 01 40 71 74 00 ⏱ Daily 10–5 Ⓜ Porte d'Auteuil).

BOIS DE BOULOGNE

An area of 845ha, 35km of paths, 150,000 trees and 300,000 bushes, plus endless distractions ranging from boating to clay-pigeon shooting and gastronomy.
➕ A/B4–6 ⏱ Permanently open 🍴 Cafés, restaurants Ⓜ Porte Dauphine, Porte d'Auteuil

JARDIN DES TUILERIES

Laid out in 1564, later radically formalised by Le Nôtre. Now replanted to match adjoining Louvre. Maillol's statues rest in the shade of chestnut trees.
➕ F/G5 ✉ Rue de Rivoli 75001 ⏱ Daily dawn–dusk 🍴 Open-air cafés Ⓜ Tuileries 🎟 Free

PARC ANDRÉ-CITROËN

A cool futurist park divided into specialist gardens, landscaped in 1980s on site of former Citroën factory.
➕ C8 ✉ Rue Balard, rue Leblanc 75015 ☎ 01 45 57 13 35 ⏱ Oct–Mar daily 9–6. Apr–Sep daily 9AM–10PM Ⓜ Balard

PARC MONCEAU

Classic park planted in 1783 by Thomas Blaikie by order of the Duc d'Orléans. Picturesque *faux* ruins, statues and Ledoux's rotunda create timeless setting.
➕ E3 ✉ Boulevard de Courcelles 75008 ☎ 01 42 27 08 64 ⏱ Oct–Mar daily 7AM–8PM. Apr–Sep daily 7AM–10PM Ⓜ Monceau

PARC MONTSOURIS

A Haussmann creation designed on English models, with copses and serpentine paths. Small lake with swans, waterfall and grotto. Summer bandstand.
➕ G10 ✉ Avenue Reille/Boulevard Jourdan 75014 ⏱ Oct–Mar daily 8:30–6. Apr–Sep daily 8:30AM–10PM 🍴 Restaurant Ⓜ RER Line B Cité Universitaire 🎟 Free

VIEWS

Don't forget superlative panoramas from
CENTRE GEORGES POMPIDOU ➤ 41
LA GRANDE ARCHE ➤ 54
INSTITUT DU MONDE ARABE ➤ 45
NOTRE-DAME ➤ 43
SACRÉ-COEUR ➤ 33
TOUR EIFFEL ➤ 26

ARC DE TRIOMPHE
Situated at the hub of Haussmann's web of 12 avenues, and the ultimate symbol of Napoleon's military pretensions and might. Video projections.
🔳 D4 ✉ Place de l'Etoile 75008 ☎ 01 43 80 31 31 ⏰ Oct–Mar daily 10–6. Apr–Sep Sun–Mon 9:30–6; Tue–Sat 9:30AM–10:30PM 🚇 Charles de Gaulle-Etoile 💷 Expensive

LA GRANDE ROUE
Dizzy, whirling views of the Tuileries and Louvre from the Big Wheel at the heart of the funfair.
🔳 G5 ✉ Rue de Rivoli 75001 ⏰ Late Jun–late Aug Sun–Fri noon–11:45; Sat noon–12:45PM 🚇 Tuileries 💷 Moderate

LA SAMARITAINE
The 10th floor at Magasin 2 offers a spectacular close-up on the city's Left Bank monuments. Lunch in the open air on the 9th floor or dine in newly designed splendour at the 5th-floor restaurant, Toupary (☎ 01 40 41 29 29 ⏰ Mon–Sat 8PM–1AM).
🔳 H6 ✉ Rue de la Monnaie 75001 ☎ 01 40 41 20 20 ⏰ Easter–Oct Mon–Wed, Fri–Sat 9:30–7; Thu 9:30AM–10PM 🍴 Cafeteria, restaurant 🚇 Pont Neuf 💷 Free

SQUARE DU VERT GALANT
Quintessential river-level view of bridges and the Louvre, shaded by willows and stunning at sunset.
🔳 G6 ✉ Place du Pont-Neuf 75001 ⏰ Oct–Mar daily 9–5:30. Apr–Sep daily 9AM–10PM 🚇 Pont Neuf

TOUR MONTPARNASSE
The 59th floor of this 209m modern tower looming over Montparnasse offers sweeping vistas. Films on Paris are screened on the 56th floor.
🔳 F8 ✉ 33 Avenue du Maine 75015 ☎ 01 45 38 52 56 ⏰ Oct–Mar daily 9:30AM–10:30PM. Apr–Sep daily 9:30AM–11:30PM 🍴 Bar, restaurant 🚇 Montparnasse-Bienvenue 💷 Expensive

Pollution over Paris

The promised views over Paris do not always materialise as the capital is often hidden in haze trapped by the saucer-like shape of the Ile de France. Measures taken since the mid-1970s have helped: in one decade industrial pollution was reduced by 50 per cent and the replacement of coal by nuclear energy and gas further cleared the air. However, carbon-monoxide levels (from vehicle exhausts) often exceed EU norms.

The view from Tour Montparnasse

CHILDREN'S ACTIVITIES

CIRQUE ALEXIS GRÜSS
Perennial favourite, with a new high-tech circus show.
🔲 A4 ✉ Allée de la Reine Marguerite, Bois de Boulogne 75016
☎ 01 45 01 53 53 🕐 Shows on Wed, Sat, Sun and public holidays
Ⓜ Pont de Neuilly 💷 Very expensive

DISNEYLAND PARIS
Disney's mega-resort struggles with financial problems but survives. Kids' paradise.
✉ 77777 Marne-la-Vallée ☎ 01 64 74 30 00. Recorded information: 01 60 30 60 30 🕐 10–6 🍴 Cafés, restaurants Ⓜ RER Line A Marne-la-Vallée-Chessy 💷 Very expensive

LA GÉODE
This cinema's hemispherical screen is designed to plunge the spectators into the action with frequent nature and science films. Near by are Le Cinaxe, a mobile cinema, and the Cité des Sciences et de l'Industrie (➤ 50), with other children's activities.
🔲 L2 ✉ 26 Avenue Corentin Cariou 75019 ☎ 01 36 68 29 30
🕐 Sessions Tue–Sun 🍴 Cafés in park Ⓜ Porte de la Villette
💷 Very expensive

JARDIN D'ACCLIMATATION
Specially designed part of the Bois de Boulogne with minitrain (leaves from Porte Maillot on Wed, Sat, Sun and public holidays), playground, fairground, educational museum, 'enchanted river', circus, zoo and puppet theatre.
🔲 B4 ✉ Bois de Boulogne 75016 ☎ 01 40 67 90 82 🕐 Daily 10–6 🍴 Café Ⓜ Les Sablons 💷 Cheap

PARC ASTÉRIX
Some 35km north of Paris is this theme park dedicated to the comic-strip hero Astérix. Plenty of animation, rides, games and food.
✉ 60128 Plailly ☎ 03 44 62 34 34
🕐 Apr–mid-Oct Mon–Fri 10–6; Sat–Sun 10–10 🍴 Cafés, restaurants Ⓜ RER Line B, Roissy-Charles de Gaulle 💷 Very expensive

Le guignol
A juvenile crowd-puller dating back to the early 19th century is the *guignol*, an open-air puppet show held in several Parisian parks. Shows are staged in summer on Wednesdays, weekends and during school holidays. Find them in parks such as the Luxembourg, Montsouris, Buttes Chaumont, Champ de Mars or the Jardin d'Acclimatation.

La Géode, Parc de la Villette

FREE ATTRACTIONS

ARÈNES DE LUTÈCE
A partly ruined Gallo-Roman amphitheatre now favoured by *boules*-playing retirees. Destroyed in AD 280, it was restored in the early 1900s.
➕ H7 ✉ Rue des Arènes 75005 🕐 Oct–Mar daily 8–5:30. Apr–Sep daily 8AM–10PM Ⓜ Jussieu

DROUOT RICHELIEU
Let yourself be tempted at Paris's main auction rooms. A Persian carpet, a Louis XV commode or a bunch of cutlery may come under the hammer. Auctions start at 2PM.
➕ G4 ✉ 9 rue Drouot 75009 ☎ 01 48 00 20 20 🕐 Daily 11–6. Closed Jul–Aug Ⓜ Richelieu-Drouot

JARDIN DU PALAIS-ROYAL
Elegant 18th-century arcades surround this peaceful formal garden and palace (now the Conseil d'Etat and the Ministère de la Culture), redolent of Revolutionary history. Daniel Buren's conceptual striped columns occupy the Cour d'Honneur.
➕ G5 ✉ Place du Palais-Royal 75001 🕐 Oct–Mar daily 7:30AM–8:30PM. Apr–Sep daily 7AM–11PM 🍴 Restaurants, tea-room Ⓜ Palais-Royal/Musée du Louvre

MÉMORIAL DE LA DÉPORTATION
In the Ile de la Cité's eastern tip is a starkly designed crypt lined with 200,000 quartz pebbles to commemorate French citizens deported by the Nazis.
➕ H6 ✉ Square de l'Ile de France 75004 🕐 Mon–Fri 8:30–5:30; Sat–Sun 9–5:30 Ⓜ Cité

PALAIS DE JUSTICE
Follow in the footsteps of lawyers, judges and crooks down echoing corridors, staircases and courtyards, and, if your French is up to it, sit in on a court case. This former royal palace took on its present function during the Revolution.
➕ H6 ✉ Boulevard du Palais 75001 ☎ 01 44 32 50 00 🕐 Mon–Fri 9–6 Ⓜ Cité

PAVILLON DE L'ARSENAL
This strikingly designed building houses well-conceived exhibitions of urban Paris alongside a permanent display of the city's architectural evolution.
➕ J7 ✉ 21 Boulevard Morland 75004 ☎ 01 42 76 33 97 🕐 Tue–Sat 10:30–6:30; Sun 11–7 Ⓜ Sully Morland

Bargain Paris

Nothing comes cheap in this city of light and the *franc fort*. Although gastronomy, official culture and history do cost money, browsing at the *bouquinistes* along the Seine, picnicking on the riverbanks, reading in the parks, exploring backstreets or spinning hours away for the cost of a coffee on a *terrasse* are some of Paris's bargains.

The Palais-Royal

59

INTRIGUING STREETS

BOULEVARD DE ROCHECHOUART
Teeming with struggling immigrants. Impromptu markets, Tati (the palace of cheap clothes), or seedy sex shops and a pervasive aroma of *merguez* and chips.
✚ H3 🚇 Barbès-Rochechouart

Cour de Rohan
A narrow cobbled passage tucked away on the Left Bank, the Cour de Rohan connects rue Saint-André-des-Arts with Boulevard Saint-Germain and dates from 1776, although it incorporates a medieval tower. It became a hive of Revolutionary activity, with Marat printing pamphlets at No 8, Danton installed at No 20 and the anatomy professor Dr Guillotin (conceptor of that 'philanthropic beheading machine') at No 9.

RUE DU CHERCHE-MIDI
César's sculpture on the rue de Sèvres crossroads marks out this typical Left Bank street, home to the famous Poîlane bakery (No 8) and the Musée Hébert (No 85). Main interest ends at the Boulevard Raspail.
✚ G7 🚇 Saint-Sulpice

RUE DU FAUBOURG SAINT-HONORÉ
Price-tags and politics cohabit in this street of luxury. See Hermès' imaginative window-dressing or salute the gendarmes in front of the Elysée Palace.
✚ F4/5 🚇 Madeleine

RUE JACOB
Antique and interior-decoration shops monopolise this picturesque stretch. Make a 20m detour to the Musée Delacroix on the delightful Place Furstemberg.
✚ G6 🚇 Saint-Germain-des-Prés

RUE MONSIEUR-LE-PRINCE
An uphill stretch lined with university bookshops, antique and ethnic shops, and a sprinkling of student restaurants. Sections of the medieval city wall are embedded in Nos 41 and 47.
✚ G7 🚇 Odéon

RUE DES ROSIERS
Effervescent street at heart of Paris's Jewish quarter. Kosher butchers and restaurants, the old hammam and Hebrew bookshops rub shoulders with designer boutiques. Quietens considerably on Saturdays.
✚ J6 🚇 Saint-Paul

Shopfront in the rue des Rosiers

RUE VIEILLE-DU-TEMPLE
The pulse of the hip Marais district, dense in bars, cafés, boutiques, and, further north, the historic Hôtel Amelot-de-Bisseuil (No 47), the Maison J Hérouët, the Hôtel de Rohan (No 87) and the garden of the Musée Picasso (► 51).
✚ J6 🚇 Saint-Paul

PARIS
where to...

LUXURY HOTELS

Expect to pay over FF1,500 for a single room in the luxury category.

Le Crillon

Whether you stay at the Ritz, the Crillon, the Meurice, the Bristol or Georges V, all have their tales to tell, but that of the Crillon is perhaps the most momentous as this family mansion (still 100 per cent French-owned by the Taittingers of champagne fame) managed to survive the Revolution despite having the guillotine on its doorstep. Mary Pickford and Douglas Fairbanks spent their honeymoon here.

LE CRILLON
An old Parisian classic which reeks glamour, history and major investments. Suites are almost the norm here.
➕ F5 ✉ 10 Place de la Concorde 75008 ☎ 01 44 71 15 00; fax 01 44 71 15 02 🚇 Concorde

L'HÔTEL
A Parisian legend redolent of Oscar Wilde's last days. Kitsch piano-bar/restaurant and some superb rooms.
➕ G6 ✉ 13 rue des Beaux Arts 75006 ☎ 01 43 25 27 22; fax 01 43 25 64 81 🚇 Saint-Germain-des-Prés

HÔTEL DU JEU DE PAUME
Delightful, small hotel carved out of a 17th-century royal tennis-court. Tasteful rooms with beams and marble bathrooms; some duplex suites. No restaurant.
➕ J7 ✉ 54 rue Saint-Louis-en-l'Île 75004 ☎ 01 43 26 14 18; fax 01 40 46 02 76 🚇 Pont Marie

HÔTEL LUTETIA
Completely refurbished in art deco style by Sonia Rykiel in 1989. Avoid the cheaper back rooms. Well-located between Saint-Germain and Montparnasse.
➕ F7 ✉ 45 Boulevard Raspail 75006 ☎ 01 49 54 46 46; fax 01 49 54 46 00 🚇 Sèvres-Babylone

HÔTEL MEURICE
Classically ornate luxury, once home to Salvador Dali and before that the Nazi HQ during the Occupation. Now efficiently run by the CIGA group.
➕ G5 ✉ 228 rue de Rivoli 75001 ☎ 01 44 58 10 10; fax 01 44 58 10 15/16 🚇 Tuileries

HÔTEL MONTALEMBERT
Fashionable Left Bank hotel with garden-patio, bar and restaurant. Chic design details, well-appointed rooms. Popular with Americans.
➕ F6 ✉ 3 rue de Montalembert 75007 ☎ 01 45 49 68 68; fax 01 45 49 69 49 🚇 Rue du Bac

HÔTEL SAINTE BEUVE
Exclusive establishment between the heart of Montparnasse and the Luxembourg gardens. Period antiques mix happily with modern furnishings.
➕ G7 ✉ 9 rue Sainte-Beuve 75006 ☎ 01 45 48 20 07; fax 01 45 48 67 52 🚇 Vavin

HÔTEL SAN RÉGIS
Convenient for the couturiers in Avenue Montaigne. Elaborately decorated but modestly scaled hotel, popular with American showbiz. Restaurant for hotel residents only.
➕ E5 ✉ 12 rue Jean Goujon 75008 ☎ 01 44 95 16 16; fax 01 45 61 05 48 🚇 Alma-Marceau

PAVILLON DE LA REINE
Set back from Place des Vosges. Flowery courtyard, tasteful period decoration and chintzy rooms.
➕ J6 ✉ 28 Place des Vosges, 75004 ☎ 01 42 77 96 40; fax 01 42 77 63 06 🚇 Chemin Vert

Mid-Range Hotels

HÔTEL DE L'ABBAYE SAINT GERMAIN
This quaint, historic establishment was once a monastery. Flowery, cobbled courtyard, elegant salons, terraced duplex rooms and friendly staff.

🔁 G7 ✉ 10 rue Cassette 75006 ☎ 01 45 44 38 11; fax 01 45 48 07 86 🚇 Saint-Sulpice

HÔTEL D'ANGLETERRE
Former British Embassy. Pretty garden-patio, spacious rooms where Hemingway once stayed. Bar and piano lounge. Book well ahead.

🔁 G6 ✉ 44 rue Jacob 75006 ☎ 01 42 60 34 72; fax 01 42 60 16 93 🚇 Saint-Germain-des-Prés

HÔTEL BERGÈRE
A 131-room hotel run by Best Western close to the Grands Boulevards. Reliable though anonymous service.

🔁 H4 ✉ 34 rue Bergère 75009 ☎ 01 47 70 34 34; fax 01 47 70 36 36 🚇 Rue Montmartre

HÔTEL DUC DE SAINT-SIMON
Rather pricey but the antique furnishings and picturesque setting just off Boulevard Saint-Germain justify it. Comfortable rooms, intimate atmosphere. Needs advance booking.

🔁 F6 ✉ 14 rue Saint-Simon 75007 ☎ 01 45 48 35 66; fax 01 45 48 68 25 🚇 Rue du Bac

HÔTEL LENOX
Popular with design and fashion world. Chase T S Eliot's ghost and enjoy the restored, stylish 1930s bar. Book well ahead.

🔁 G6 ✉ 9 rue de l'Université 75007 ☎ 01 42 96 10 95; fax 01 42 61 52 83 🚇 Rue du Bac

HÔTEL DES MARRONIERS
Named after the chestnut trees that dominate the garden. Obsessively vegetal/floral-based decoration. Oak-beamed rooms; vaulted cellars converted to lounges. Book well ahead

🔁 G6 ✉ 21 rue Jacob 75006 ☎ 01 43 25 30 60; fax 01 40 46 83 56 🚇 Saint-Germain-des-Prés

HÔTEL MOLIÈRE
On a quiet street near the Louvre and Opéra. Well-appointed, reasonably priced rooms, and helpful staff.

🔁 G5 ✉ 21 rue Molière 75001 ☎ 01 42 96 22 01; fax 01 42 60 48 68 🚇 Pyramides

HÔTEL LA PERLE
Renovated 17th-century building on a quiet street near Saint-Germain. Charming breakfast patio, bar, well-appointed rooms.

🔁 G6 ✉ 14 rue des Canettes 75006 ☎ 01 43 29 10 10; fax 01 46 34 51 04 🚇 Mabillon

RÉSIDENCE LORD BYRON
Comfortable, classy 31-room hotel just off the Champs-Elysées. Small garden and well-appointed, reasonably priced rooms.

🔁 E4 ✉ 5 rue Châteaubriand 75008 ☎ 01 43 59 89 98; fax 01 42 89 46 04 🚇 Georges V

A moderately priced hotel will charge FF500–1,000 for a single room.

Three-star rating
All these three-star establishments are obvious favourites with business travellers, so it is virtually impossible to find rooms during trade-fair seasons such as May–early June and mid-September–October. In summer many offer discounts as their clientele shrinks. All rooms are equipped with colour TV, direct-dial phone, private bath or shower-rooms, mini-bar and most with hair-drier. Air-conditioning is not standard, but lifts are common.

BUDGET ACCOMMODATION

You should be able to find a single room in a budget hotel for under FF500.

Budget hotels

Gone are the heady days when Paris was peppered with atmospheric one-star hotels with their inimitable signs *'eau à tous les étages'* ('water on every floor'). Now there are bath- or shower-rooms in every bedroom, and correspondingly higher prices and smaller rooms. So don't expect to swing cats in budget hotel rooms, but do expect breakfast and receptionists who speak a second language in every hotel with two or more stars.

GRAND HÔTEL MALHER
Recently renovated family hotel with 31 well-equipped rooms; excellent location.
🚇 J6 ✉ 5 rue Malher 75004 ☎ 01 42 72 60 92; fax 01 42 72 25 37 🚇 Saint-Paul

GRAND HÔTEL DE SUEZ
Fifty-room hotel in central location on busy boulevard. Good value but lacks atmosphere.
🚇 H6 ✉ 31 Boulevard Saint-Michel 75005 ☎ 01 46 34 08 02; fax 01 40 51 79 44 🚇 Cluny-La Sorbonne

HÔTEL ANDRÉ GILL
Charming courtyard setting on quiet side-street close to Pigalle. Renovated rooms, reasonably priced.
🚇 G3 ✉ 4 rue André Gill 75018 ☎ 01 42 62 48 48; fax 01 42 62 77 92 🚇 Pigalle

HÔTEL DU COLLÈGE DE FRANCE
Tranquil 29-roomed establishment near the Sorbonne. Some 6th-floor rooms offer a glimpse of Notre-Dame.
🚇 H7 ✉ 7 rue Thénard 75005 ☎ 01 43 26 78 36; fax 01 46 34 58 29 🚇 Maubert-Mutualité

HÔTEL ESMERALDA
A very popular doll's-house hotel near Notre-Dame. Reasonably priced; book well ahead.
🚇 H6 ✉ 4 rue Saint-Julien-le-Pauvre 75005 ☎ 01 43 54 19 20; fax 01 40 51 00 68 🚇 Saint-Michel

HÔTEL ISTRIA
Legendary Mont-parnasse hotel once frequented by Rilke, Duchamp and Man Ray. Twenty-six atmospheric rooms and friendly staff.
🚇 G8 ✉ 29 rue Campagne Première 75014 ☎ 01 43 20 91 82; fax 01 43 22 48 45 🚇 Raspail

HÔTEL JARDIN DES PLANTES
Pretty hotel overlooking botanical gardens. Good facilities.
🚇 H7 ✉ 5 rue Linné 75005 ☎ 01 47 07 06 20; fax 01 47 07 62 74 🚇 Jussieu

HÔTEL KENSINGTON
Convenient for the Eiffel Tower and Champ de Mars. An up-market address for a pleasant little hotel with fully renovated rooms.
🚇 E6 ✉ 79 Avenue de la Bourdonnais 75007 ☎ 01 47 05 74 00; fax 01 47 05 25 81 🚇 Ecole-Militaire

HÔTEL LINDBERGH
Modernised hotel on a tranquil side-street near busy crossroads and the shops of Saint-Germain. Well-equipped rooms and polyglot staff.
🚇 F7 ✉ 5 rue Chomel 75007 ☎ 01 45 48 35 53; fax 01 45 49 31 48 🚇 Sèvres-Babylone

HÔTEL LION D'OR
Small family hotel with adequately modernised rooms and very helpful staff. Good value for its central location.
🚇 G5 ✉ 5 rue de la Sourdière 75001 ☎ 01 42 60 79 04; fax 01 42 60 09 14 🚇 Tuileries

HÔTEL MICHELET-ODÉON
Reasonable rates and quiet location next to

Théâtre de l'Odéon. No frills, but helpful service.
🏨 G7 ✉ 6 Place de l'Odéon 75006 ☎ 01 46 34 27 80; fax 01 46 34 55 35 Ⓜ Odéon

HÔTEL DE LA PLACE DES VOSGES

Charming 17th-century townhouse in a quiet street close to Place des Vosges. Basic comforts, excellent location.
🏨 J6 ✉ 12 rue Birague 75004 ☎ 01 42 72 60 46; fax 01 42 72 02 64 Ⓜ Bastille

HÔTEL PRIMA-LEPIC

In cleaner air up the hill of Montmartre, this bright hotel has well-decorated but smallish rooms and a courtyard-style reception area.
🏨 G3 ✉ 29 rue Lepic 75018 ☎ 01 46 06 44 64; fax 01 46 06 66 11 Ⓜ Abbesses

HÔTEL RÉCAMIER

Flowery wallpaper in this tranquil, friendly little hotel close to Saint-Germain and Luxembourg gardens.
🏨 G7 ✉ 3 bis Place Saint-Sulpice 75006 ☎ 01 43 26 04 89 Ⓜ Saint-Sulpice

HÔTEL DE ROUEN

Very cheap 22-room hotel with surprisingly well-equipped rooms. Central location near the Louvre and Palais-Royal.
🏨 G5 ✉ 42 rue Croix-des-Petits-Champs 75001 ☎ 01 42 61 38 21 Ⓜ Louvre-Rivoli

HÔTEL DU 7E ART

Cinephile's hotel decorated with movie photos and memorabilia. Great location and reasonably priced rooms.
🏨 J6 ✉ 20 rue Saint-Paul

75004 ☎ 01 42 77 04 03; fax 01 42 77 69 10 Ⓜ Saint-Paul

HÔTEL SOLFÉRINO

A rare budget hotel in the chic 7th. Antique furniture. Opposite Musée d'Orsay on quiet street. Excellent value.
🏨 F6 ✉ 91 rue de Lille 75007 ☎ 01 47 05 85 54; fax 01 45 55 51 16 Ⓜ Solférino

HÔTEL DE LA SORBONNE

On quiet side-street near the Sorbonne. Small but comfortable rooms. Well established and unpretentious.
🏨 H7 ✉ 6 rue Victor-Cousin 75005 ☎ 01 43 54 58 08; fax 01 40 51 05 18 Ⓜ Cluny-La Sorbonne

HÔTEL DU VIEUX SAULE

In a quiet street in north of Marais. Modernised, with reasonable facilities.
🏨 J5 ✉ 6 rue de Picardie 75003 ☎ 01 42 72 01 14; fax 01 40 27 88 21 Ⓜ Filles du Calvaire

SUPER HÔTEL

Near Père Lachaise cemetery. Excellent value, easy transport, comfortable rooms.
🏨 M5 ✉ 208 rue des Pyrénées 75020 ☎ 01 46 36 97 48; fax 01 46 36 26 10 Ⓜ Gambetta

TIMHÔTEL LE LOUVRE

One of small chain with reliable amenities and reasonably priced rooms. Well situated for Louvre and Les Halles.
🏨 G5 ✉ 4 rue Croix-des-Petits-Champs 75001 ☎ 01 42 60 34 86; fax 01 42 60 10 39 Ⓜ Louvre-Rivoli

Bed and breakfast

Bed-and-breakfast systems now exist which fix up visitors with host families. Try France Lodge (☎ 01 53 20 02 54; fax 01 53 20 01 25) or International Café Couette (☎ 01 42 94 92 00; fax 01 42 94 93 12). For those who want to stay longer and rent furnished accommodation the best source is the free classified ads magazine *France-USA Contacts* (*FUSAC*). It is available at English bookshops and student travel agencies.

HAUTE CUISINE

The restaurants on the following pages are in three price categories:

£££ over FF400 per person

££ up to FF400 per person

£ up to FF120 per person

French mean cuisine

'The only cooks in the civilised world are French. Other races have different interpretations of food. Only the French mean *cuisine* because their qualities – rapidity, decision-making, tact – are used. Who has ever seen a foreigner succeed in making a white sauce?'

– Nestor Roqueplan (1804–70), Editor of *Le Figaro*.

Rose-tinted dining

Le Pré Catalan (£££) has an outdoor setting near the rose gardens of the Parc Bagatelle. Excellent seasonal dishes and exquisite desserts. (⊠ Bois de Boulogne, Route de Suresnes 75016 ☎ 01 44 14 41 14).

ALAIN DUCASSE (£££)

Former Robuchon temple of Parisian *nouvelle cuisine*, now masterminded by Alain Ducasse from Monaco.
➕ C5 ⊠ 59 Avenue Raymond Poincaré 75116 ☎ 01 47 27 12 27 ◷ Closed Sat–Sun, Jul ◉ Trocadéro

LE BRISTOL (£££)

Uniquely elegant 18th-century oval-shaped restaurant, renowned for exquisite seafood and impeccable service.
➕ E4 ⊠ 112 rue du Faubourg Saint-Honoré 75008 ☎ 01 42 66 91 45 ◷ Daily ◉ Miromesnil

LE GRAND VEFOUR (£££)

Superb late 18th-century setting under arcades of Palais-Royal, with ghosts of Napoleon, Colette and Sartre. Classic French cuisine. Relatively reasonably priced lunch menu.
➕ G5 ⊠ 17 rue du Beaujolais 75001 ☎ 01 42 96 56 27 ◷ Closed Sat–Sun, Aug ◉ Palais-Royal/Musée du Louvre

GUY SAVOY (£££)

One of Paris's top young chefs continues to surprise with contrasting flavours and textures. Efficient service and contemporary décor.
➕ D4 ⊠ 18 rue Troyon 75017 ☎ 01 43 80 40 61 ◷ Closed Sat–Sun ◉ Charles de Gaulle-Etoile

LASSERRE (£££)

A favourite with foreign visitors; impeccable service and cuisine. An extra is the sliding roof.
➕ E5 ⊠ 17 Avenue Franklin-D Roosevelt 75008 ☎ 01 43 59 53 43 ◷ Closed Sun, Mon lunch, Aug ◉ Franklin-D Roosevelt

LUCAS-CARTON (£££)

Majorelle's art nouveau décor is the haunt of the dressy rich and famous. Try the roast pigeon with coriander.
➕ F5 ⊠ 9 Place de la Madeleine 75008 ☎ 01 42 65 22 90 ◷ Closed Sat–Sun, Aug, 24 Dec–3 Jan ◉ Madeleine

MICHEL ROSTANG (£££)

Rostang still holds his own in the Parisian gastronomy stakes with interesting combinations, and superb cheeses and desserts. Elegant table-settings.
➕ D3 ⊠ 20 rue Rennequin 75017 ☎ 01 47 63 40 77 ◷ Closed Sun ◉ Ternes

TAILLEVENT (£££)

Intimate restaurant with a confirmed reputation – advance booking is essential. Inventive cuisine – try the curried ravioli snails. Superlative wine list.
➕ E4 ⊠ 15 rue Lamennais 75008 ☎ 01 45 63 39 94 ◷ Closed Sat–Sun, Aug, public holidays ◉ Georges V

LA TOUR D'ARGENT (£££)

Legendary sanctuary of *canard au sang* but lighter dishes do exist. Fabulous view over the Ile Saint-Louis, warm atmosphere and great wine cellar.
➕ H7 ⊠ 15–17 Quai de la Tournelle 75005 ☎ 01 43 54 23 31 ◷ Closed Mon ◉ Maubert-Mutualité

REGIONAL FRENCH RESTAURANTS

AUBERGE BRESSANE (£/££)

Delectable dishes from eastern France and an impressive wine list of Bordeaux and Burgundies. Excellent-value lunch menus. Mock medieval décor.

🔢 E6 ✉ 16 Avenue de la Motte Picquet 75007 ☎ 01 47 05 98 37 🕐 Closed Sat lunch 🚇 Latour-Maubourg

LA BARACANE (££)

Tiny, tastefully decorated restaurant whose menu homes in on Gascony and ducks. Reasonably priced though limited choice in the set lunch/dinner.

🔢 J6 ✉ 38 rue des Tournelles 75004 ☎ 01 42 71 43 33 🕐 Closed Sat lunch, Sun 🚇 Bastille

BRASSERIE FLO (££)

Spectacular Alsatian brasserie which dishes up mountains of delicious *choucroute spéciale*. Noisy, popular and chaotic.

🔢 H4 ✉ 7 Cour des Petites Ecuries 75010 ☎ 01 42 46 15 00 🕐 Daily until 1AM 🚇 Château d'Eau

LE CAVEAU DU PALAIS (££)

A wonderful old classic; long-time favourite with Yves Montand and Simone Signoret. Homely regional cooking.

🔢 G6 ✉ 17/19 Place Dauphine 75001 ☎ 01 43 26 04 28 🕐 Closed Sat, Sun 🚇 Pont Neuf

CHEZ BENOIT (£££)

Long-standing favourite; classic regional dishes. Booking advisable.

🔢 H5 ✉ 20 rue Saint-Martin 75004 ☎ 01 42 72 25 76 🕐 Daily 🚇 Rambuteau

LE CLODENIS (££)

Intimate, discreet restaurant which serves aromatic Provençal dishes.

🔢 G2 ✉ 57 rue Caulaincourt 75018 ☎ 01 46 06 20 26 🕐 Closed Sun–Mon 🚇 Lamarck-Caulaincourt

LE COUDE FOU (££)

Popular Marais bistro with excellent wine list and hearty classics.

🔢 J6 ✉ 12 rue du Bourg-Tibourg 75004 ☎ 01 42 77 15 16 🕐 Closed Sun lunch 🚇 Hôtel de Ville

LE CROQUANT (££)

Reworks classic dishes of the south-west. Sublime *confit de canard*.

🔢 C8 ✉ 28 rue Jean-Maridor 75015 ☎ 01 45 58 50 83 🕐 Closed Sun eve, Mon 🚇 Lourmel

AUX FINS GOURMETS (££)

Somewhat faded 1920s splendour, but serves copious portions of Basque and Béarnais cuisine.

🔢 F6 ✉ 213 Boulevard Saint-Germain 75007 ☎ 01 42 22 06 57 🕐 Closed Sun, Mon lunch 🚇 Rue du Bac

LOUIS LANDES (££)

A warm atmosphere and a menu of traditional dishes from the south-west. Monthly dinners based around a theme; wine-tastings.

🔢 F9 ✉ 157 Avenue du Maine 75014 ☎ 01 45 43 08 04 🕐 Closed Sat lunch, Sun 🚇 Mouton-Duvernet

Alsace and the south-west

Gastronomically speaking, Alsace and the south-west are probably the best-represented regions in Paris. Numerous brasseries churn out *choucroute* (sauerkraut), but it is the south-west which carries off the prizes with its variations on goose and duck. Recent research has found that inhabitants of this region have unexpectedly low rates of cardiac disease – despite their daily consumption of cholesterol-high *foie gras*.

ASIAN & ITALIAN RESTAURANTS

ASIAN

L'AFGHANI (£)
Tucked away in the heights of Montmartre. Wonderfully authentic Afghan food.

🚩 H3 ✉ 16 rue Paul-Albert 75018 ☎ 01 42 51 08 72 🕐 Daily 🚇 Château Rouge

BHAI BHAI SWEETS (£)
In a dilapidated covered passageway in the hub of Paris's Little India. Not as spicy-hot as it could be, but tasty curries nonetheless.

🚩 H4 ✉ 77 Passage Brady 75010 ☎ 01 42 46 77 29 🕐 Daily 🚇 Strasbourg Saint-Denis

CHEZ ROSINE (££)
Orchestrated by charismatic Rosine Ek from Cambodia. Succulent, imaginative dishes. Sophisticated.

🚩 G5 ✉ 12 rue du Mont Thabor 75001 ☎ 01 49 27 09 23 🕐 Closed Sun, Mon lunch 🚇 Tuileries

CHIENG-MAI (££)
Elegant Thai restaurant. Subtle flavours (fish steamed in banana-leaf, grilled spicy mussels) and charming service.

🚩 H7 ✉ 12 rue Frédéric-Sauton 75005 ☎ 01 43 25 45 45 🕐 Closed Sun, part of Aug 🚇 Maubert-Mutualité

HAWAÏ (£)
Huge, animated canteen-style restaurant, popular with local Chinese. Generous soups, Southeast Asian specialities.

🚩 J10 ✉ 87 Avenue d'Ivry 75013 ☎ 01 45 86 91 90 🕐 Daily 🚇 Porte d'Ivry

KAPPA (££)
Family-style Japanese *sushi* restaurant. Animated, warm atmosphere.

🚩 G6 ✉ 6 rue des Ciseaux 75006 ☎ 01 43 26 33 31 🕐 Closed Sun 🚇 Saint-Germain-des-Prés

LAO SIAM (£)
Wide selection of Southeast Asian cuisines: giant prawns sautéed in ginger and chives, or whole crab cooked in coconut milk and chilli pepper.

🚩 K4 ✉ 49 rue de Belleville 75011 ☎ 01 40 40 09 68 🕐 Daily 🚇 Belleville

LE NIOULLAVILLE (£)
Vast, kitsch Hong Kong-style restaurant with a long menu of Chinese, Laotian, Thai and Vietnamese specialities.

🚩 K4 ✉ 32–4 rue de l'Orillon 75011 ☎ 01 43 38 95 23 🕐 Closed Sun evening 🚇 Belleville

PATTAYA (£)
Unpretentious, with outside tables in summer. Delicious prawn and lemon-grass soup and other Thai dishes.

🚩 H5 ✉ 29 rue Etienne-Marcel 75001 ☎ 01 42 33 98 09 🕐 Daily 🚇 Les Halles

PHÖ DONG-HUONG (£)
Popular Vietnamese family 'canteen' which serves generous soups, seafood and meat dishes. Bustling atmosphere; distinct smoking and no-smoking sections.

🚩 K4 ✉ 14 rue Louis Bonnet 75011 ☎ 01 43 57 42 81 🕐 Closed Tue 🚇 Belleville

The 13th arrondissement

The Parisian Chinese community is concentrated in Belleville, where it coexists with Arabs and Africans; in the 3rd *arrondissement*, where invisible sweat-shops churn out cheap leather goods; and above all in the 13th *arrondissement* (🚇 Tolbiac, Porte d'Ivry). Here, Chinese New Year is celebrated with dragon parades in late January to early February. Gastronomically speaking it offers a fantastic array of Indochinese and Chinese restaurants and soup kitchens – all at budget prices.

TAN DINH (££)

Up-market Vietnamese cuisine, in an elegantly designed restaurant just behind the Musée d'Orsay. Impressive wine list and polished service.

➕ F6 ✉ 60 rue de Verneuil 75007 ☎ 01 45 44 04 84
🕒 Closed Sun 🚇 Rue du Bac

YAMAMOTO (£)

Super-fresh *sushi* and excellent-value set lunches. Popular, so crowded until 2PM. Less animated in the evening.

➕ G5 ✉ 6 rue Chabanais 75002 ☎ 01 49 27 96 26
🕒 Closed Sun 🚇 Bourse

YUGARAJ (££)

One of Paris's best Indian restaurants. Discreet, elegant atmosphere, friendly Sri Lankan waiters, excellent-value 'Delhi-Express' lunch menu.

➕ G6 ✉ 14 rue Dauphine 75006 ☎ 01 43 26 44 91
🕒 Closed Mon lunch 🚇 Pont Neuf

ITALIAN

CASA BINI (££)

Chic but relaxed, a favourite with Catherine Deneuve. Carpaccio and Tuscan dishes are specialities.

➕ G6 ✉ 36 rue Grégoire de Tours 75006 ☎ 01 46 34 05 60 🕒 Closed Sat, Sun lunch 🚇 Odéon

L'ENOTECA (££)

Colourfully designed up-market Italian restaurant/wine bar in the Marais. The buffet of *antipasti* is delicious and the pasta dishes are refined.

➕ J6 ✉ 25 rue Charles V 75004 ☎ 01 42 78 91 44
🕒 Daily 🚇 Saint-Paul

PASTAVINO (£)

Bresaola and choice of three freshly prepared pasta dishes every day. Clean contemporary design; cheerful service.

➕ G6 ✉ 55 rue Dauphine 75006 ☎ 01 46 33 93 83
🕒 Daily 🚇 Odéon

SIPARIO (££)

Theatrically styled restaurant convenient for Bastille Opera house. Wide and inventive choice of pasta, seafood and meat dishes.

➕ K7 ✉ 69 rue de Charenton 75011 ☎ 01 43 45 70 26
🕒 Closed Sun 🚇 Bastille

STRESA (££)

Fashionable isn't the word. Local couturiers drop in here for a quick pasta, risotto or plate of divine *antipasti*. Run with gusto by Neapolitan identical twins. Book ahead.

➕ E5 ✉ 7 rue de Chambiges 75008 ☎ 01 47 23 51 62
🕒 Closed Sat, Sun 🚇 Alma-Marceau

AUX TROIS CANETTES (££)

A friendly and old-fashioned establishment plastered with nostalgic views of Naples. Extensive menu of authentic Italian classics – polenta, ossobucco, sardines.

➕ G6 ✉ 18 rue des Canettes ☎ 01 44 07 03 02 🕒 Closed Sat lunch, Sun 🚇 Mabillon

Panini reigns

It is said that Cathérine de Médicis, the Italian wife of Henri II, invented French cuisine in the 16th century – though Gallic opinions may differ. Italian cuisine in 20th-century Paris is, not surprisingly, very much a pizza-pasta affair, and authentic dishes are rare. However, the latest in snack fashions is the toasted *panini*, oozing mozarella and tomatoes, especially popular with businessmen near the Bourse (Stock Exchange).

ARAB RESTAURANTS

Couscous and tajine

Couscous is a mound of steamed semolina which is accompanied by a tureen of freshly cooked vegetables (onion, tomato, carrot, potato, courgette) and the meat (or not) of your choice, from grilled lamb kebabs (*brochettes*) to chicken or *merguez* (spicy sausages). *Tajine* is a delicious all-in-one stew, traditionally cooked in a covered terracotta dish, which may combine lamb and prunes or chicken, pickled lemon and olives.

AL DAR (££)
Luxurious but over air-conditioned restaurant, highly regarded by the Lebanese community. Take-away section.
✚ H7 ✉ 8/10 rue Frédéric Sauton 75005 ☎ 01 43 25 17 15 🕐 Daily Ⓜ Maubert-Mutualité

L'ATLAS (££)
Fabulous kitsch juxtaposition of Louis XIII chairs and Moroccan mosaics. The diverse menu includes 12 types of *couscous*, pigeon and other specialities, all served with genuine smiles.
✚ H7 ✉ 12 Boulevard Saint-Germain 75005 ☎ 01 46 33 86 98 🕐 Daily Ⓜ Maubert-Mutualité

CAFÉ MODERNE (£)
Generous *couscous* and *tajines* as well as basic steaks and fish, and a choice of North African or French wines. 1930s décor.
✚ K6 ✉ 19 rue Keller 75011 ☎ 01 47 00 53 62 🕐 Closed Sun Ⓜ Bastille

LES CÈDRES DU LIBAN (£)
A Lebanese institution with reasonable prices. Friendly service, and excellent *taboulé*, hummus and spicy meat dishes.
✚ F7 ✉ 5 Avenue du Maine 75014 ☎ 01 42 22 35 18 🕐 Daily Ⓜ Montparnasse-Bienvenue

CHEZ OMAR (£)
Generous *couscous* and grilled meats in a friendly, spacious and buzzing setting. Popular, so book for dinner or arrive early.
✚ J5 ✉ 47 rue de Bretagne 75003 ☎ 01 42 72 36 26 🕐 Closed Sun lunch Ⓜ Arts et Métiers

DARKOUM (££)
Refined Moroccan cuisine – seafood, *pastilla*, *couscous* and *tajines* – served in a spacious Arabian Nights-style interior.
✚ G5 ✉ 44 rue Sainte-Anne 75002 ☎ 01 42 96 83 76 🕐 Closed Sat lunch Ⓜ Bourse

LE MANSOURIA (££)
Elegant décor and aromatic *tajines*, although it gets overcrowded on Saturdays.
✚ L7 ✉ 11 rue Faidherbe 75011 ☎ 01 43 71 00 16 🕐 Closed Sun, Mon lunch Ⓜ Faidherbe-Chaligny

NOURA (££)
Up-market busy Lebanese snack-bar with take-away service, brother of the plush Pavillon Noura (☎ 01 47 20 33 33) down the road.
✚ D4 ✉ 27 Avenue Marceau 75116 ☎ 01 47 23 02 20 🕐 Daily Ⓜ Charles de Gaulle-Etoile

TIMGAD (£££)
Spectacular Moorish décor. Delicate *pastilla*, perfect *couscous* and attentive service. Booking recommended.
✚ D4 ✉ 21 rue Brunel 75017 ☎ 01 45 74 23 70 🕐 Daily Ⓜ Argentine

BRASSERIES & BISTROS

LE BALZAR (££)
Fashionable brasserie near the Sorbonne. Seafood, pigs' trotters, *cassoulet*. Camus and Sartre had their last argument here.
H7 ✉ 49 rue des Ecoles 75005 ☎ 01 43 54 13 67 🕐 Closed Aug Ⓜ Cluny-La Sorbonne

BOFINGER (££)
Claims to be Paris's oldest brasserie (1864). Soaring glass dome, mirrored interior, chandeliers, and seafood, *choucroute* and steaks.
K6 ✉ 5 rue de la Bastille 75004 ☎ 01 42 72 87 82 🕐 Daily Ⓜ Bastille

BRASSERIE STELLA (££)
Original 1950s décor in heart of the chic 16th *arrondissement*. Seafood, oysters, and wines from Sancerre and Beaujolais.
C5 ✉ 133 Avenue Victor Hugo 75016 ☎ 01 47 27 80 54 🕐 Daily Ⓜ Victor Hugo

CHEZ PAUL (££)
A mecca for Bastille art-dealers and artists; essential to book. Delicious stuffed rabbit, *steak tartare*. Mediocre service
K6 ✉ 13 rue de Charonne 75011 ☎ 01 47 00 34 57 🕐 Daily Ⓜ Ledru-Rollin

LA COUPOLE (££)
A Montparnasse institution dating from the 1920s. Wide choice of brasserie food, reasonable late-night menu (after 11PM).
F7 ✉ 102 Boulevard du Montparnasse 75014 ☎ 01 43 20 14 20 🕐 Daily Ⓜ Vavin

LE DROUOT (£)
Art deco canteen belonging to the more famous Chartier (along the road). It is far easier to find a table here and the food is equally good value.
G5 ✉ 103 rue de Richelieu 75002 ☎ 01 42 96 68 23 🕐 Daily Ⓜ Richelieu-Drouot

LE GRAND COLBERT (££)
Restored 19th-century brasserie opening on to the Galerie Colbert. Good seafood and a cheerful atmosphere.
G5 ✉ 2 rue Vivienne 75002 ☎ 01 42 86 87 88 🕐 Daily Ⓜ Bourse

AU PETIT RICHE (££)
Wonderful old 1880s bistro. Reliable traditional cuisine and good Loire wines.
G4 ✉ 25 rue Le Peletier 75009 ☎ 01 47 70 68 68 🕐 Closed Sun Ⓜ Richelieu-Drouot

LE PETIT SAINT-BENOÎT (£)
Popular old Saint-Germain classic; décor barely changed since the 1930s. Outside tables in the summer.
G6 ✉ 4 rue Saint-Benoît 75006 ☎ 01 42 60 27 92 🕐 Closed Sat, Sun Ⓜ Saint-Germain-des-Prés

AU VIEUX CHÊNE (£)
Pleasantly aged bistro east of the Bastille. Excellent-value traditional dishes, friendly service.
L7 ✉ 7 rue du Dahomey 75011 ☎ 01 43 71 67 69 🕐 Closed Sun Ⓜ Faidherbe-Chaligny

La Coupole

Horror struck Parisian hearts in the mid-1980s when it was announced that La Coupole had been bought by property developers and several floors were to be added on top. This happened, but the famous old murals (by Juan Gris, Soutine, Chagall, Delaunay and many more) have been reinstated, the red-velvet seats preserved and the art deco lights duly restored. The 1920s décor is now classified as a historic monument.

SALONS DE THÉ

Mariage-Frères

It's hard to escape from Mariage-Frères without making a minor investment in their tastefully presented products – whether a decorative tin of obscure Japanese green tea, a Chinese teapot, a tea-brick or a delicately tea-scented candle. The Mariage brothers started importing tea to France back in 1854. The choice now extends to over 400 varieties, so that reading the menu becomes an exotic excursion through India to the Far East.

ANGÉLINA (££)
Overpriced and overrated lunches, but exquisite cakes and hot chocolate make it a favourite for tea. Proustian Belle Epoque décor.
⊞ G5 ✉ 226 rue de Rivoli 75001 ☎ 01 42 60 82 00 ⏰ Closed evenings, Aug Ⓜ Tuileries

BERNARDAUD (££)
Latest designer tea-rooms signed by Olivier Gagnère. Tea and cakes served on Limoges porcelain.
⊞ F4 ✉ 8 bis Galerie Royale 75008 ☎ 01 42 66 22 55 ⏰ Mon–Sat 8:30AM–7PM Ⓜ Madeleine

LES ENFANTS GÂTÉS (£)
Comfortable armchairs, plants and pictures. Good choice of teas, fruit juices, salads, tarts and cakes. Fills up fast at the weekend for brunches.
⊞ J6 ✉ 43 rue des Francs-Bourgeois 75004 ☎ 01 42 77 07 63 ⏰ Daily until 7:30PM Ⓜ Rambuteau

LADURÉE (££)
Rides on the back of an illustrious past and local luxury shops. Avoid the overpriced lunches. Tea and cakes under a ceiling fresco of a cherubic pastry chef.
⊞ F5 ✉ 18 rue Royale 75008 ☎ 01 42 60 21 79 ⏰ Closed Sun, Aug Ⓜ Concorde

LE LOIR DANS LA THÉIÈRE (£)
Established local favourite. Salads, vegetable tarts, cakes, and plenty of tea and fruit juices.
⊞ J6 ✉ 3 rue des Rosiers 75004 ☎ 01 42 72 90 61 ⏰ Daily until 7PM Ⓜ Saint-Paul

MARIAGE-FRÈRES (££)
Chic, discreet tea-shop with an elegant upstairs tea-room perfect for non-smoking tête-à-têtes over divine cakes or Sunday brunch. Its sibling is in the Marais (✉ 30/32 rue du Bourg Tibourg 75004 ☎ 01 42 72 28 11).
⊞ G6 ✉ 13 rue des Grands Augustins 75006 ☎ 01 40 51 82 50 ⏰ Daily until 7:30PM Ⓜ Odéon

LA PAGODE (£)
Exotic tea-room attached to an extraordinary cinema housed in an ornate Chinese pagoda. Overlooks a small Japanese garden.
⊞ F6 ✉ 57 bis rue de Babylone 75007 ☎ 08 36 68 75 07 ⏰ Afternoons daily Ⓜ Saint-François-Xavier

A PRIORI THÉ (££)
A favourite with the fashion crowd. Book at lunch. Light lunches, teas, American cakes.
⊞ G5 ✉ 36 Galerie Vivienne 75002 ☎ 01 42 97 48 75 ⏰ Daily until 7PM Ⓜ Bourse

TCH'A (£)
Sells 40 varieties of Chinese tea and serves delicious light lunches. Traditional service, aesthetic décor.
⊞ G6 ✉ 6 rue du Pont de Lodi 75006 ☎ 01 43 29 61 31 ⏰ Closed Mon Ⓜ Pont Neuf

MISCELLANEOUS RESTAURANTS

MA BOURGOGNE (££)
Perfect for a summer lunch or dinner. Hearty, unpretentious food or just stop for a drink.
⊞ J6 ✉ 19 Place des Vosges 75004 ☎ 01 42 78 44 64
⊙ Daily. Closed Feb
🚇 Chemin Vert

CAFÉ DE L'INDUSTRIE (£)
Spacious, relaxed café-restaurant-tea-room open until 1:30AM. Whiffs of 1930s, rock music, and reasonable though basic food.
⊞ K6 ✉ 16 rue Saint-Sabin 75011 ☎ 01 47 00 13 53
⊙ Closed Sat 🚇 Bastille

AUX CHARPENTIERS (££)
Solid French cuisine in a popular neighbourhood restaurant dedicated to the carpenters' guild. Daily specialities.
⊞ G6 ✉ 10 rue Mabillon 75006 ☎ 01 43 26 30 05
⊙ Daily 🚇 Mabillon

LA GALERIE (£)
Pleasant relief from the tourist haunts of Montmartre. Very good-value set lunch and dinner menus which may include salmon ravioli or duck with cherries. Cheerful and friendly.
⊞ G3 ✉ 16 rue Tholozé 75018 ☎ 01 42 59 25 76
⊙ Closed Sun 🚇 Abbesses

JOE ALLEN (£)
Reliable hamburger-based fare served with humour and background music in a still fashionable late-night haunt in Les Halles.
⊞ H5 ✉ 30 rue Pierre Lescot

75001 ☎ 01 42 36 70 13
⊙ Daily 🚇 Etienne-Marcel

ORESTIAS (£)
Pushy, lively, Greek restaurant. Good value, above all the giant shoulder of lamb. Highlight is the chandelier.
✉ G6 ✉ 4 rue Grégoire de Tours 75006 ☎ 01 43 54 62 01 ⊙ Closed Sun 🚇 Odéon

LA POTÉE DES HALLES (£/££)
Famed for its delicious potée (a steaming pot of stewed meat and vegetables) and other regional dishes. Exceptional Belle Epoque interior.
⊞ H5 ✉ 3 rue Etienne-Marcel 75001 ☎ 01 42 36 18 68
⊙ Closed Sat lunch, Sun
🚇 Etienne-Marcel

PRUNIER (£££)
Recently refurbished to return to former art deco splendour. Glamorous clientele indulges in excellent fresh seafood specialities prepared under the accomplished eye of a former Taillevent director.
⊞ D4 ✉ 16 Avenue Victor Hugo 75016 ☎ 01 44 17 35 85 ⊙ Closed Sun eve, Mon
🚇 Charles de Gaulle-Etoile

WILLI'S WINE BAR (££)
Cheerful, British-owned restaurant-wine bar with extensive international wine list. Fresh French cuisine plus the inimitable Cambridge dessert.
⊞ G5 ✉ 13 rue des Petits Champs 75001 ☎ 01 42 61 05 09 ⊙ Closed Sun 🚇 Palais-Royal/Musée du Louvre

Pharamond

Alexandre Pharamond served his first plate of *tripes à la mode de Caen* in 1870, two doors from the site of the present restaurant. After he moved to No 24 the restaurant was entirely redecorated for the 1900 Exposition Universelle, and most of this structure and decoration has been preserved. The pretty floral and vegetal friezes which cover the walls of the rooms once adorned the entire four-floor façade. A sanctuary for lovers of tripe, pigs' trotters and *andouillette*. Prices are high and booking is essential (⊞ H5 ✉ 24 rue de la Grande Truanderie 75001 ☎ 01 42 33 06 72 ⊙ Closed Mon lunch, Sun, Jul 🚇 Les Halles).

DEPARTMENT STORES & DESIGNER BOUTIQUES

DEPARTMENT STORES

BHV (BAZAR DE L'HÔTEL DE VILLE)

The do-it-yourself mecca. Browse among the basement nuts and bolts, choose paint or have wood cut on the 5th floor.

➕ H6 ✉ 52/64 rue de Rivoli 75004 ☎ 01 42 74 90 00 🕐 Mon–Tue, Thu–Sat 9:30–7; Wed 9:30AM–10PM Ⓜ Hôtel de Ville

AU BON MARCHÉ RIVE GAUCHE

Very *BCBG* ('*bon chic bon genre*'). Gourmet-food department, designer clothes, household linens, haberdashery and excellent bookshop.

➕ F7 ✉ 22 rue de Sèvres 75007 ☎ 01 44 39 80 00 🕐 Mon–Sat 9:30–7 Ⓜ Sèvres-Babylone

GALERIES LAFAYETTE

Under a giant glass dome, an enticing display of everything a home and its inhabitants need. Marginally better quality and pricier than Printemps. Top fashion designers are all represented and accessories are endless. Smaller branch by the Tour Montparnasse.

➕ G4 ✉ 40 Boulevard Haussmann 75009 ☎ 01 42 82 34 56 🕐 Mon–Wed, Fri–Sat 9:30–6:45; Thu 9:30–9 Ⓜ Chaussée d'Antin

MARKS & SPENCER

Food, clothes, household goods and excellent wines. Another branch of this very British chain store is at 35 Boulevard Haussmann 75009.

➕ H6 ✉ 88 rue de Rivoli 75004 ☎ 01 44 61 08 00 🕐 Mon–Fri 10–8, Sat 10–7:30 Ⓜ Châtelet, Hôtel de Ville

PRINTEMPS

A classic for men's and women's fashions, accessories, household goods, furniture, designer gadgets and more. Budget-conscious fashion victims should look for the store's own collection: Sélection Printemps.

➕ G4 ✉ 64 Boulevard Haussmann 75009 ☎ 01 42 82 50 00 🕐 Mon–Wed, Fri–Sat 9:35–7; Thu 9:35AM–10PM Ⓜ Havre-Caumartin

SAMARITAINE

Labyrinthine department with main store in Magasin II, a superb 1904 construction. Good basement hardware section. Fashion is so-so, but toy department is a paradise for kids. Useful separate store for sports equipment and clothes.

➕ H6 ✉ 19 rue de la Monnaie 75001 ☎ 01 40 41 20 20 🕐 Mon–Wed, Fri–Sat 9:30–7; Thu 9:30AM–10PM Ⓜ Pont Neuf

DESIGNER BOUTIQUES

AGNÈS B

Pioneering designer who now rests on her comfortable reputation. Her shops monopolise most of this street. Still a favourite for her unchanging classics, but fabrics and cut are no longer what they were.

Opening hours

Parisian opening hours follow a Monday–Saturday pattern. Smaller shops generally open by 10AM, sometimes closing for lunch, and shut at 7PM. Avoid shopping on Saturdays, when every citizen seems to hit the streets, and take advantage of department store late-opening nights. Chain-stores such as Prisunic and Monoprix are useful for picking up inexpensive household goods and even fashion accessories.

Children's and men's clothes too.
✚ H5 ✉ 1–6 rue du Jour 75001 ☎ 01 45 08 56 56 Ⓜ Les Halles

AMELIA MENDES
Interesting fabrics and cuts; young and chic label by KYO, who also designs for Dior and Scherrer at much less affordable prices.
✚ G5 ✉ 8 rue de la Vrillière 75001 ☎ 01 42 61 07 30 Ⓜ Bourse

BARBARA BUI
Silky flowing fabrics in subtle colours, well-cut suits and a superbly designed boutique by Pucci de Rossi. One of Paris's most talented young designers.
✚ H5 ✉ 23 rue Etienne-Marcel 75001 ☎ 01 40 26 43 65 Ⓜ Etienne-Marcel

CHANTAL THOMASS
Paris's sexiest clothes shop, suspiciously reminiscent of an up-market brothel. Frills and thrills, stockings, lacy lingerie and some equally seductive clothes.
✚ G5 ✉ 1 rue Vivienne 75001 ☎ 01 40 15 01 36 Ⓜ Bourse

DOROTHÉE BIS
Classically imaginative knitwear in colourful, supple styles, popular with a more mature avant-garde clientèle.
✚ H5 ✉ 46 rue Etienne-Marcel 75002 ☎ 01 42 21 04 00 Ⓜ Les Halles

IRIÉ
Former assistant of Kenzo who creates superbly cut and accessibly priced separates. A pioneer in this discreet street.
✚ G6 ✉ 8 rue du Pré-aux-Clercs 75007 ☎ 01 42 61 18 28 Ⓜ Saint-Germain-des-Prés

KASHIYAMA
Look out for the label of Martin Margiela, a rising star from Antwerp who worked for Gaultier and now designs his own version of the avant-garde.
✚ G6 ✉ 147 Boulevard Saint-Germain 75006 ☎ 01 46 34 11 50 Ⓜ Saint-Germain-des-Prés

LOLITA LEMPICKA
Established inventive chic, very Parisienne. Ultra-feminine details and shop design.
✚ J6 ✉ 3 bis rue des Rosiers 75004 ☎ 01 42 74 42 94 Ⓜ Saint-Paul

MICHEL KLEIN
Reliably chic from season to season. Search out the Klein d'Oeil label which offers very feminine designs for smaller budgets – but not as small as all that.
✚ G6 ✉ 6 rue du Pré-aux-Clercs 75007 ☎ 01 47 03 93 76 Ⓜ Saint-Germain-des-Prés

ROMEO GIGLI
Venetian carnival invades an old printers' workshop. Gigli's rich velvet, taffeta, silk and jersey designs are presented like works of art, which they are. Men's creations on mezzanine.
✚ J6 ✉ 46 rue de Sévigné 75004 ☎ 01 48 04 57 08 Ⓜ Saint-Paul

Fashion hubs
The fact that women's high fashion is concentrated in just three epicentres makes clothes shopping, or mere window-gazing, easy. The hub of Place des Victoires (home to Kenzo, Stephane Kélian, Plein Sud and Victoire) continues along the rue Etienne-Marcel and towards Les Halles. The Marais' enticing offerings run between the rue de Sévigné, rue des Rosiers, Place des Vosges and side-streets. Saint-Germain burgeons along and off the boulevard, rue de Grenelle and continues up the Boulevard Raspail.

Zen cuts
Issey Miyake reigns OK! His sculptural, finely pleated creations in imaginative synthetics are sold at 3 Place des Vosges 75004 (☎ 01 48 87 01 86), but Plantation/Issey Miyake at 17 Boulevard Raspail 75007 (☎ 01 45 48 12 32) is where more accessible designs are available. And if black and white is your style, head for Yohji Yamamoto at 25 rue du Louvre 75001 (☎ 01 42 21 42 93) for sober geometric cuts for men and women.

MARKETS

Food markets

Parisians shop daily for ultra-fresh produce and perfectly oozing cheeses. Circulating food markets spring up on boulevards throughout the city on different days of the week (the Bastille Sunday market is particularly enormous), but permanent food markets exist in rue Poncelet (🔢 D3), rue Daguerre (🔢 G/F8) and in rue de Buci on the Left Bank (🔢 G6). All keep provincial lunch hours, so avoid 1–4PM.

CARREAU DU TEMPLE
A covered market specialising in leather goods. Bargain hard and you may pay half the usual price.
🔢 J5 ✉ Rue E Spuller 75003 🕐 Tue–Sun 9–noon 🚇 Temple

MARCHÉ D'ALIGRE
Second-hand clothes, crockery and bric-à-brac huddle in the middle of a large, low-priced food market.
🔢 K7 ✉ Place d'Aligre 75012 🕐 Tue–Sun 8–1 🚇 Ledru-Rollin

MARCHÉ DE MONTREUIL
Jeans and jackets start at the métro, but persevere across the bridge for domestic appliances, carpets, bric-à-brac and some great second-hand stuff. Morning is best.
🔢 N6 ✉ Avenue de la Porte de Montreuil 75020 🕐 Sat–Mon 7–6 🚇 Porte de Montreuil

MARCHÉ AUX OISEAUX
Caged birds whistle and chirp for new owners every Sunday. During the week (except Mon) feathered friends make way for a flower market.
🔢 H6 ✉ Place Louis Lépine 75004 🕐 Sun 9–7 🚇 Cité

MARCHÉ AUX PUCES DE SAINT-OUEN
(➤ 42)

MARCHÉ DE LA RUE LEPIC
Up a steep hill, but worth the effort. Head down the other side of the hill to the rue du Poteau (🔢 G/H2 🚇 Jules-Joffrin) for African foods.
🔢 G3 ✉ Rue Lepic 75018 🕐 Tue–Sat 9–1, 4–7; Sun 9–1 🚇 Abbesses

MARCHÉ DE LA RUE MONTORGUEIL
The leftovers of Les Halles food market, now a marble-paved pedestrian street with atmosphere and plenty of trendy little bars and lunch places.
🔢 H5 ✉ Rue Montorgueil 75001 🕐 Tue–Sat 9–1, 4–7; Sun 9–1 🚇 Les Halles

MARCHÉ DE LA RUE MOUFFETARD
A tourist classic straggling down a winding, hilly street. Wonderful array of fruit and vegetables, and plenty of aromatic cheeses and charcuterie. Good café stops *en route*.
🔢 H8 ✉ Rue Mouffetard 75005 🕐 Tue, Thu, Sat 9–1, 4–7 🚇 Monge

MARCHÉ AUX TIMBRES
Philatelists zoom in here to buy and sell their miniature treasures.
🔢 E5 ✉ Rond-Point des Champs-Elysées 75008 🕐 Thu, Sat, Sun and holidays 9–7 🚇 Franklin-D Roosevelt

MARCHÉ DE VANVES
A favourite with young yuppies and hot on 1950s and deco styles. Second-hand furniture, bric-à-brac, paintings, prints and some ethnic stands.
🔢 E9 ✉ Avenue Georges Lafenestre, Avenue Marc Sangnier 75014 🕐 Sat–Sun 7–7:30 🚇 Porte de Vanves

ART & ANTIQUES

ARTCURIAL

Large store of contemporary art (prints, jewellery, sculpture, carpets) and an excellent art bookshop.

✠ E4 ✉ 9 Avenue Matignon 75008 ☎ 01 42 99 16 16 🕓 Tue–Sat 10:30–7:15 🚇 Franklin-D Roosevelt

CARRÉ RIVE GAUCHE

This grid of streets is home to some of Paris's top antique dealers. Archaeological pieces, Louis XIV, XV, Empire, Japanese scrolls, 19th-century bronzes, astrolabes, prints – it's all here.

✠ G6 ✉ Rue du Bac, Quai Voltaire, rue des Saints-Pères, rue de l'Université 75007 🕓 Tue–Sat 10:30–7 🚇 Rue du Bac

GALERIE DOCUMENTS

Original posters and etchings from 1890 to 1940 by such masters as Toulouse-Lautrec and Mucha. Mail-order service.

✠ G6 ✉ 53 rue de Seine 75006 ☎ 01 43 54 50 68 🕓 Tue–Sat 10:30–12:30, 2:30–7 🚇 Odéon

GALERIE DURAND-DESSERT

Spectacular conversion of an old Bastille mattress factory into a conceptual art mecca.

✠ K6 ✉ 28 rue de Lappe 75011 ☎ 01 48 06 92 23 🕓 Tue–Sat 11–7 🚇 Bastille

GALERIE DU JOUR AGNÈS B

Fashion meets art at Agnès B's gallery. Young, hip talent in painting and photography.

✠ H5 ✉ 6 rue du Jour 75001 ☎ 01 42 33 43 40 🕓 Tue–Sat 11–7 🚇 Les Halles

GALERIE MONTENAY

A long-standing contemporary art gallery, where young French and foreign artists are regularly exhibited.

✠ G6 ✉ 31 rue Mazarine 75006 ☎ 01 43 54 85 30 🕓 Tue–Sat 11–1, 2:30–7 🚇 Odéon

LOUVRE DES ANTIQUAIRES

Huge, modernised complex of antique shops which sell everything from Eastern carpets to Lalique glass, jewellery, furniture, silver, porcelain and paintings. High prices.

✠ G5 ✉ 2 Place du Palais-Royal 75001 ☎ 01 42 97 27 00 🕓 Tue–Sun 11–7 🚇 Palais-Royal/Musée du Louvre

VILLAGE SAINT-PAUL

A cluster of antique and bric-à-brac shops opening onto an enclosed square. Shops continue down the streets on either side, with everything from Asian textiles to glass, old furniture or clothes.

✠ J6 ✉ Rue Saint-Paul, rue Charlemagne 75004 🕓 Thu–Mon 11–7 🚇 Saint-Paul

VILLAGE SUISSE

Network of up-market furniture and antique shops in a chic residential area.

✠ D7 ✉ 54 Avenue de la Motte-Piquet, 78 Avenue de Suffren 75015 ☎ 01 43 06 69 90 🕓 Thu–Sun 10:30–7 🚇 La Motte-Piquet

Galleries

Even if you cannot afford to invest in contemporary art, Paris offers a good window on the latest movements. Art has traditionally centred on the Left Bank around the rue de Seine, but today the more avant-garde galleries spread east from the Centre Georges Pompidou area through the Marais to the Bastille. Pick up a free gallery map at one of the galleries and follow the creative route.

BOOKS & RECORDS, DESIGN & INTERIOR, FOOD & WINE

Sunday openings

Sundays now have a strong consumer itch to them at the new marble-clad Carrousel du Louvre, perfect for a rainy day. Offerings include a Virgin record/bookshop, a newsagent with a wide international selection, Bodum kitchenware, Nature et Découvertes (a fashionably 'ecological' toy and gadget shop), a stylish optician and various boutiques. The entrance is from 99 rue de Rivoli or by the Carrousel arch in the Louvre.

BOOKS & RECORDS

BRENTANO'S

Well-stocked American bookshop with good travel and art sections at the back. Bilingual staff.
➕ G5 ✉ 37 Avenue de l'Opéra 75001 ☎ 01 42 61 52 50 Ⓜ Opéra

LA CHAMBRE CLAIRE

Excellent photography bookshop with wide range of international publications. Occasional exhibitions.
➕ G7 ✉ 14 rue Saint-Sulpice 75006 ☎ 01 46 34 04 31 Ⓒ Mon–Sat Ⓜ Odéon

FNAC

The main branch of this firmly established cultural chain. Books, records, cameras, hi-fis, computer accessories. Fair-price policy reigns and staff are helpful.
➕ G7 ✉ 136 rue de Rennes 75006 ☎ 01 49 54 30 00 Ⓜ Saint-Sulpice

GALIGNANI

Pleasantly traditional, spacious bookshop brimming with laden tables and shelves. Large stock of English, German and French literature and artbooks.
➕ G5 ✉ 224 rue de Rivoli 75001 ☎ 01 42 60 76 07 Ⓜ Tuileries

LA HUNE

Excellent literary bookshop with extensive art and architecture section. Both French and imported books. Great for late-night browsing, with weekday opening until midnight.
➕ G6 ✉ 170 Boulevard Saint-Germain 75006 ☎ 01 45 48 35 85 Ⓜ Saint-Germain-des-Prés

LIBRAIRIE DES FEMMES

A feminist bookshop with a vast choice of international women writers. Next to the Saint-Germain market.
➕ G6 ✉ 74 rue de Seine 75006 ☎ 01 43 29 50 75 Ⓜ Odéon

VIRGIN MEGASTORE

Enormous palace of records with generous opening hours. Chic café. Another branch is in the Carrousel du Louvre, 99 rue de Rivoli (➕ G5).
➕ E4 ✉ 52/60 Champs-Elysées 75008 ☎ 01 49 53 50 00 Ⓒ Mon–Thu 10AM–midnight; Fri–Sat 10AM–1AM; Sun noon–midnight Ⓜ Franklin-D Roosevelt

DESIGN & INTERIOR

DEHILLERIN

A foodie's paradise, brimming with copper pans, knives, bains-maries, sieves and more. Mail-order service.
➕ H5 ✉ 18 rue de la Coquillière 75001 ☎ 01 42 36 53 13 Ⓜ Les Halles

EN ATTENDANT LES BARBARES

Colourful hive of primitive-baroque designer objects, from resin candlesticks to funky furniture by young French designers.
➕ H5 ✉ 50 rue Etienne-Marcel 75001 ☎ 01 42 33 37 87 Ⓜ Sentier

ETAMINE

Vast home-interior shop with superb objects and fabrics imported from all over the world, but firmly stamped with Parisian taste.

⊞ F6 ✉ 63 rue du Bac 75007
☎ 01 42 22 03 16
Ⓜ Rue du Bac

SOULEIADO

Cheerful range of fabrics, table-linen and cushions in bright, sunny Provençal prints.

⊞ G6 ✉ 78 rue de Seine
75006 ☎ 01 43 54 62 25
Ⓜ Mabillon

FOOD & WINE

ANDROUET

Encyclopaedic range of pungent French cheeses in perfectly ripened states. Cheese restaurant attached; delivery service in Paris.

⊞ F3 ✉ 41 rue d'Amsterdam
75008 ☎ 01 48 74 26 90
Ⓜ Liège

FAUCHON

The gourmet's paradise – at a price. Established luxury delicatessen offering only the best in spices, exotic fruit, tea, coffee, charcuterie, pâtisseries…and more.

⊞ F5 ✉ 26 Place de la
Madeleine 75008 ☎ 01 47 42
60 11 Ⓜ Madeleine

IZRAËL

Colourful souk spilling North African and Middle Eastern goodies onto pavement. Sacks of grains, bottles of spices, piles of African baskets.

⊞ J6 ✉ 30 rue François Miron
75004 ☎ 01 42 72 66 23
Ⓜ Saint-Paul

LEGRAND FILLES ET FILS

Fine wines and selected groceries in a shop dating from 1890. Helpful advice, wide price range but reliable quality. Occasional wine-tastings.

⊞ G5 ✉ 1 rue de la Banque
75002 ☎ 01 42 60 07 12
Ⓜ Bourse

LA MAISON DU MIEL

Countless types of honey – chestnut, lavender, pine-tree, acacia – presented in a pretty, tiled interior dating from 1908.

⊞ F4 ✉ 24 rue Vignon 75009
☎ 01 47 42 26 70
Ⓜ Madeleine

A LA MÈRE DE FAMILLE

Original 18th-century grocery shop with shelves laden with imaginatively created chocolates, sweets, jams and unusual groceries.

⊞ H4 ✉ 35 rue du Faubourg
Montmartre 75009 ☎ 01 47 70
83 69 Ⓜ Le Peletier

ROBERT LABEYRIE

Specialises in products from the Landes. Goose and duck livers, *foie gras*, truffles, dried mushrooms of all types.

⊞ H5 ✉ 6 rue Montmartre
75001 ☎ 01 45 08 95 26
Ⓜ Les Halles

TACHON

Unpretentious old-fashioned cheese shop, renowned for its goat, sheep and cow products.

⊞ G5 ✉ 38 rue de Richelieu
75001 ☎ 01 42 96 08 66
Ⓜ Palais-Royal/Musée du
Louvre

Ethnic attractions

Foodies suffering from a surfeit of delectable but outrageously priced French groceries should head for Paris's ethnic areas. For Indian products the Passage Brady (⊞ H4) is unbeatable, while the nearby rue d'Enghien harbours several Turkish grocery shops. Belleville offers both Arab and Chinese specialities, while the Goutte d'Or (Barbès) focuses on Africa. For a real taste of the Far East go to the Chinese supermarket Tang Frères at 47 Avenue d'Ivry in the 13th *arrondissement* (⊞ J9).

MISCELLANEOUS & OFFBEAT

Window-shopping

Some Parisian streets do not fit any convenient slot and so make for intriguing window-shopping. Try rue Jean-Jacques Rousseau and Passage Véro-Dodat (⊞ G/H5), rue Saint-Roch (⊞ G5), rue Monsieur-le-Prince and the parallel rue de l'Odéon (⊞ G7), rue Saint-Sulpice, rue des Francs-Bourgeois and rue du Pont-Louis-Philippe (⊞ J6), or rue de la Roquette (⊞ K/L6). For luxury goods take a stroll along the rue du Faubourg Saint-Honoré (⊞ E4–G5).

ANTHONY PETO
The male answer to Marie Mercié. Inventive and wearable men's quality headgear from top-hats to berets, aimed at the young and hip.
⊞ G5 ⊠ 12 rue Jean-Jacques Rousseau 75001 ☎ 01 42 21 47 15 ⓢ Louvre-Rivoli

LES ARCHIVES DE LA PRESSE
Treasure trove of old magazines, newspapers and catalogues.
⊞ J6 ⊠ 51 rue des Archives 75003 ☎ 01 42 72 63 93 ⓢ Rambuteau

L'ART DU BUREAU
High-tech and designer accessories for the desktop, tasteful stationery.
⊞ J6 ⊠ 47 rue des Francs Bourgeois 75004 ☎ 01 48 87 57 97 ⓢ Saint-Paul

AXIS
Witty contemporary objects, plates, teapots, jewellery and clocks. Another shop is at the Bastille, 13 rue de Charonne (⊞ K6).
⊞ G6 ⊠ 18 rue Guénégaud 75006 ☎ 01 43 29 66 23 ⓢ Odéon

CHÉRI-BIBI
Amusing and inventive women's hats at very affordable prices. Bit of a trek but worth it.
⊞ K6 ⊠ 82 rue de Charonne 75011 ☎ 01 43 70 51 72 ⓢ Charonne

CHRISTIAN TORTU
Anemones, amaryllis and apple-blossom… the ultimate bouquet from Christian Tortu's florist shops. Wrapping is in understated brown paper bound with raffia.
⊞ G6 ⊠ 6 Carrefour de l'Odéon 75006 ☎ 01 43 26 02 56 ⓢ Odéon

CUISINOPHILE
Tiny little shop packed with decorative old kitchen utensils, mostly in working order.
⊞ J6 ⊠ 28 rue du Bourg Tibourg 75004 ☎ 01 40 29 07 32 ⓢ Hôtel de Ville

DEBAUVE & GALLAIS
Original wood-panelled 18th-century pharmacy which developed into a chocolate shop when the medicinal properties of cocoa were discovered.
⊞ G6 ⊠ 30 rue des Saints-Pères 75007 ☎ 01 45 48 54 67 ⓢ Saint-Germain-des-Prés

DIDIER LUDOT
Rare vintage designer clothes (Chanel, Dior, Balmain) and classic Hermès handbags. Picturesque location.
⊞ G5 ⊠ 24 Galerie Montpensier ☎ 01 42 96 06 56 ⓢ Palais-Royal/Musée du Louvre

DIPTYQUE
For over 30 years this boutique has sold its own perfumed candles and *eaux de toilette*. Also men's ties, scarves and superb glasses.
⊞ H7 ⊠ 34 Boulevard Saint-Germain 75005 ☎ 01 43 26 45 27 ⓢ Maubert-Mutualité

L'HABILLEUR
End of designer lines at huge discounts. Plenty of choice, with helpful sales staff.
⊞ J5 ⊠ 44 rue de Poitou 75003 ☎ 01 48 87 77 12 ⓢ Saint-Sébastien-Froissart

IKUO

Tiny little shop, a treasure chest of interesting jewellery, mainly by Japanese creators. Good value.

⊞ G6 ✉ 11 rue des Grands Augustins 75006 ☎ 01 43 29 56 39 Ⓜ Pont Neuf

JEAN LAPORTE

An aromatic universe of pot-pourris, essences, candles and perfumes based on floral, fruity and spicy themes.

⊞ F6 ✉ 84 bis rue de Grenelle 75007 ☎ 01 45 44 61 57 Ⓜ Rue du Bac

MARIE MERCIÉ

Compulsive creator of extravagant hats. Choose your headgear here or in her original shop near Les Halles at 56 rue Tiquetonne (⊞ I15).

⊞ G7 ✉ 23 rue Saint-Sulpice 75006 ☎ 01 43 26 45 83 Ⓜ Mabillon

MI-PRIX

Designer numbers at a fraction of the price, including shoes by Michel Perry.

⊞ C8 ✉ 27 Boulevard Victor 75015 ☎ 01 48 28 42 48 Ⓜ Porte de Versailles

MOUTON À CINQ PATTES

Cut-price designer clothes packed into a crowded shop. Another branch is at 15 rue Vieille du Temple (⊞ J6).

⊞ G6 ✉ 19 rue Grégoire des Tours 75006 ☎ 01 43 29 73 56 Ⓜ Odéon

NAÏLA DE MONBRISON

Gallery showing some of the most sought-after contemporary jewellery designers' work: Marcial Berro, Tina Chow, Mattia Bonetti.

⊞ F6 ✉ 6 rue de Bourgogne 75007 ☎ 01 47 05 11 15 Ⓜ Varenne

PAPIER +

Wonderful emporium of quality paper in endless subtle hues. Superbly bound books, files, and bouquets of coloured pencils.

⊞ J6 ✉ 9 rue du Pont Louis-Philippe 75004 ☎ 01 42 77 70 49 Ⓜ Pont Marie

SCOOTER

To get that real Les Halles look, drop in here for the latest accessories: ethnic, 1960s/70s revival transformed into jewellery, bags, clothes.

⊞ H5 ✉ 10 rue de Turbigo 75001 ☎ 01 45 08 89 31 Ⓜ Les Halles

SI TU VEUX

Charming and affordable toy shop with interesting toys, games and dressing-up gear. Separate section devoted to teddy bear-related items.

⊞ G5 ✉ 68 Galerie Vivienne 75002 ☎ 01 42 60 59 97 Ⓜ Bourse

TATI

Originally aimed at the emptiest purses in Paris, Tati now attracts the rich and famous but is still cheap. Women's, men's and children's clothes, as well as household goods.

⊞ H3 ✉ 2–30 Boulevard Rochechouart 75018 ☎ 01 42 55 13 09 Ⓜ Barbès-Rochechouart

Chocaholics

Chocolate came to Europe via Spain from South America. Under Louis XIV it became a fashionable drink and was served three times a week at Versailles. Paris's first chocolate shop opened in 1659. Voltaire drank up to 12 cups a day and Napoleon apparently had a penchant for it first thing in the morning. But with their consumption of a mere 5.5kg per person per annum, the French lag behind the Swiss, who consume an annual 10kg, and the Belgians at 7kg.

CONCERT VENUES, JAZZ CLUBS & NIGHTCLUBS

Cheap concerts

Numerous classical music concerts are held in churches – try Saint-Eustache, Saint-Germain-des-Prés, St-Julien-le-Pauvre, Saint-Louis-en-l'Ile, Saint-Roch and Saint-Séverin. Seats are reasonably priced and the quality of music is sometimes very high. In May–September free concerts are held in parks all over the city. Programmes are available at the Office du Tourisme or the Hôtel de Ville, or ☎ 01 40 71 76 47.

Recitals

The most prestigious venue on the classical-buff's circuit, now home to the Orchestre de Paris, is the Salle Pleyel (✉ 252 rue du Faubourg Saint-Honoré ☎ 01 45 61 53 00). Chopin gave his last recital here and it is the venue for many of Paris's major concerts, often with world-famous soloists, and for radio and record recordings. Another established concert hall, the Salle Gaveau, still attracts top international opera singers and pianists despite of its shabby appearance (✉ 45 rue de la Boétie 75008 ☎ 01 49 53 05 07).

CONCERT VENUES

AUDITORIUM DES HALLES

Lunchtime and early evening concerts and recitals: classical, world-music, jazz.
✚ H5 ✉ Forum des Halles, Porte Sainte-Eustache 75001 ☎ 01 42 36 13 90 ⓠ Les Halles

CITÉ DE LA MUSIQUE

Accessible classical, jazz, world-music at this new concert hall in a rather out-of-the-way location.
✚ L2 ✉ 221 Avenue Jean-Jaurès 75019 ☎ 01 44 84 44 84 ⓠ Porte de Pantin

OPÉRA BASTILLE

Long-term teething problems continue at Paris's 'people's' opera house. Opera, recitals, dance and even theatre.
✚ K6 ✉ 120 rue de Lyon 75012 ☎ 01 44 73 13 00 ⓠ Bastille

OPÉRA COMIQUE

Sumptuously decorated opera house which stages light opera, dance and sometimes theatre.
✚ G4 ✉ 5 rue Favart 75002 ☎ 01 42 44 45 46 ⓠ Richelieu-Drouot

THÉÂTRE DES CHAMPS-ELYSÉES

Top international orchestras play in a high-priced, stately setting.
✚ E5 ✉ 15 Avenue Montaigne 75008 ☎ 01 49 52 50 50 ⓠ Alma-Marceau

THÉÂTRE DU CHÂTELET

Varied programme of opera, symphonic music and dance. Cheap seats at lunchtime.
✚ H6 ✉ Place du Châtelet 75001 ☎ 01 40 28 28 40 ⓠ Châtelet

THÉÂTRE DE LA VILLE

Modern theatre with an adventurous programme of contemporary dance, avant-garde music, theatre and early evening recitals of world-music.
✚ H6 ✉ Place du Châtelet 75004 ☎ 01 42 74 22 77 ⓠ Châtelet

JAZZ CLUBS

BILBOQUET

Strait-laced crowd with good sprinkling of tourists. Traditional jazz, pricey cocktails. Restaurant.
✚ G6 ✉ 13 rue Saint-Benoît 75006 ☎ 01 45 48 81 84 ⓠ Saint-Germain-des-Prés

CAVEAU DE LA HUCHETTE

Still going strong, a smoky basement bar with dancing and live jazz from 9:30PM.
✚ H6 ✉ 5 rue de la Huchette 75005 ☎ 01 43 26 65 05 ⓠ Saint-Michel

CHAPELLE DES LOMBARDS

Funky Bastille haunt with a hot atmosphere; Caribbean, raï (Algerian rock) and rap music; open until dawn.
✚ K6 ✉ 19 rue de Lappe 75011 ☎ 01 43 57 24 24 ⓣ Thu–Sat ⓠ Bastille

NEW MORNING

One of Paris's top jazz/blues/soul bars. Good atmosphere,

dedicated crowd, quality assured. Top names require booking.

➕ H4 ✉ 7/9 rue des Petites Ecuries 75010 ☎ 01 45 23 56 39 Ⓜ Château d'Eau

PETIT OPPORTUN
Classic jazz venue in Les Halles featuring live bands from 10:30PM. Reasonable food.

➕ H6 ✉ 15 rue des Lavandières-Sainte-Opportun 75001 ☎ 01 42 36 01 36 🕐 Closed Sun Ⓜ Châtelet

LE SUNSET
Part of the Les Halles cluster, a restaurant-bar with good jazz concerts from 10PM until the small hours. Reasonably priced food.

➕ H6 ✉ 60 rue des Lombards 75001 ☎ 01 40 26 46 60 Ⓜ Châtelet

LA VILLA
Top jazz names. Sleekly designed cocktail-bar setting in stylish post-modern hotel basement, open late. Book.

➕ G6 ✉ 29 rue Jacob 75006 ☎ 01 43 26 60 00 🕐 Closed Sun Ⓜ Saint-Germain-des-Prés

NIGHTCLUBS

L'ARC
Fairly up-market club with selective door policy. Piano-bar restaurant and interior garden.

➕ D4 ✉ 12 rue de Presbourg 75016 ☎ 01 45 00 45 00 🕐 From 11:30PM nightly Ⓜ Charles de Gaulle-Etoile

LES BAINS
Still number one for fashion and showbiz set. Heavy door-policing;

restaurant. Go very late.

➕ H5 ✉ 7 rue du Bourg-l'Abbé 75003 ☎ 01 48 87 01 80 🕐 Nightly Ⓜ Etienne-Marcel

LE BALAJO
Over 60 years old, ritzy 1930s décor; mainly disco, techno and funk.

➕ K6 ✉ 9 rue de Lappe 75011 ☎ 01 47 00 07 87 🕐 Wed–Sat Ⓜ Bastille

LE BATACLAN
An old favourite now rejuvenated. Fashion-media set; fancy dress on Fridays, mainly house music on Saturdays.

➕ K5 ✉ 50 Boulevard Voltaire 75011 ☎ 01 47 00 30 12, 47 00 55 22 🕐 Thu–Sat from 11PM Ⓜ Oberkampf

PIGALL'S
Latest Pigalle haunt which thunders soul, acid-jazz. Transvestites add to the funkiness.

➕ G3 ✉ 77 rue Pigalle 75009 ☎ 01 46 27 82 82 🕐 Thu–Sat from 12PM Ⓜ Pigalle

RÉGINE
Flashy mature crowd, rich in media stars. Careful grooming expected, so look smart – you may be lucky.

➕ E4 ✉ 49–51 rue de Ponthieu 75008 ☎ 01 43 59 21 13 Ⓜ Franklin-D Roosevelt

LE TANGO
Unpretentious club with hot-blooded Afro-Latino rhythms, tango, salsa, reggae and soul.

➕ J5 ✉ 13 rue au Maire 75003 ☎ 01 42 72 17 78 🕐 Fri–Sat from 11PM Ⓜ Arts et Métiers

Clubs and raves

Paris clubbing is both serious and fickle – serious because no truly cool Parisian turns up before midnight, and fickle because mass loyalties change rapidly. Most clubs keep going through the night until dawn, and nearly all charge for entry on Friday and Saturday nights (this usually includes a drink). For one-off raves, theme nights and house parties outside Paris, with shuttles laid on, check *Pariscope*'s English section or key in to Minitel 3615 Party News

BARS & SPECIAL CINEMAS

BARS

BAR DU MARCHÉ
Hip watering-hole with good sounds and cheerful service. Nice outdoor terrace in summer.
⊞ G6 ✉ 75 rue de Seine 75006 ☎ 01 43 26 55 15
🕙 Daily 8AM–1AM 🚇 Odéon

BAR ROMAIN
Original 1905 décor brightens this bar-restaurant, popular with a more mature showbiz crowd. Choice of over 200 cocktails.
⊞ G4 ✉ 6 rue de Caumartin 75009 ☎ 01 47 42 98 04
🕙 Mon–Sat 12PM–2AM
🚇 Havre-Caumartin

BIRDLAND
An old Saint-Germain favourite. Relaxed atmosphere, with great jazz records.
⊞ G6 ✉ 8 rue Princesse 75006 ☎ 01 43 26 97 59
🕙 Nightly 7PM–6AM
🚇 Mabillon

LES BOUCHONS
Late-night basement bar with occasional live jazz. Cheerful restaurant upstairs.
⊞ H6 ✉ 19 rue des Halles 75001 ☎ 01 42 33 28 73
🕙 Nightly 11:30PM–dawn
🚇 Châtelet

CAFÉ CANNIBALE
Relaxed, spacious and popular café in a burgeoning neighbourhood near Belleville. World-music sounds in the revived baroque interior.
⊞ K5 ✉ 93 rue Jean-Pierre Timbaud 75011 ☎ 01 49 29 95 59 🕙 Daily 🚇 Couronnes

CAFÉ CHARBON
Hip café-bar with budget snacks in lofty mirrored interior. Read the papers here until 2AM.
⊞ K5 ✉ 109 rue Oberkampf 75011 ☎ 01 43 57 55 13
🕙 Daily 🚇 Parmentier

CAFÉ NOIR
Popular late-night haunt on fringe of Les Halles. High-decibel rock and unmistakable technicolour exterior.
⊞ H5 ✉ 65 rue Montmartre 75002 ☎ 01 40 39 07 36
🕙 Daily 7:30AM–2AM. Closed Sun 🚇 Sentier

LA CASBAH
Moorish-styled bar with dancing, fancily dressed bar staff, great cocktails and décor, but very unfriendly bouncers.
⊞ K7 ✉ 18 rue de la Forge-Royale 75011 ☎ 01 43 71 71 89 🕙 Wed–Sat 11:30PM onwards 🚇 Faidherbe-Chaligny

CHINA CLUB
Shady red-lacquered bar-restaurant peopled by Mao-style waiters. Hip and crowded; avoid the food, go for a drink. Another bar upstairs.
⊞ K7 ✉ 50 rue de Charenton 75012 ☎ 01 43 43 82 02
🕙 Nightly 7PM–2AM
🚇 Ledru-Rollin

HARRY'S BAR
Old pub atmosphere. Rowdy, mature, well-tanked-up crowd.
⊞ G5 ✉ 5 rue Daunou 75002 ☎ 01 42 61 71 14 🕙 Nightly 10:30PM–4AM 🚇 Opéra

JACQUES MÉLAC
Inexpensive French wines by the glass or

Cinephile's paradise

Though French film production dropped below the 100 mark in 1994, the capital is still a cinephile's paradise. With some 350 films on offer each day, the choice can be tantalising. Foreign films shown in their original languages have 'VO' (*version originale*) after the title. New films come out on Wednesdays, which is also the day for all-round reductions. Gaumont and UGC cinemas offer multiple-entry cards which can be used for up to three people and save precious francs.

bottled for you from the barrel.

🚇 L6 ✉ 42 rue Léon Frot 75011 ☎ 01 43 70 59 27 🕐 Closed Sat–Sun and mid-Jul–mid-Aug 🚇 Charonne

MAYFLOWER

Lively, reasonably priced bar-pub that has attracted student nighthawks for years.

🚇 H7 ✉ 49 rue Descartes 75005 ☎ 01 43 54 56 47 🕐 Daily 7ᴀᴍ–2ᴀᴍ 🚇 Cardinal Lemoine

LE MOLOKO

Cavernous, popular bar on two floors. Loud rock but you can still talk.

🚇 G3 ✉ 26 rue Fontaine 75009 ☎ 01 48 74 50 26 🕐 Daily 9:30ᴘᴍ–6ᴀᴍ 🚇 Blanche

LA TARTINE

An old daytime classic. French wines by the glass, cold platters of charcuterie and cheese.

🚇 J6 ✉ 24 rue de Rivoli 75004 ☎ 01 42 72 76 85 🕐 8.30ᴀᴍ–10ᴘᴍ. Closed Tue and Aug 🚇 Hôtel de Ville

LE TRAIN BLEU

Striking Belle Epoque setting which functions as a restaurant-bar. The food is pricey, so stick to drinks only.

🚇 K7 ✉ 1st floor, Gare de Lyon 75012 ☎ 01 43 43 09 06 🕐 Daily 9ᴀᴍ–11ᴘᴍ 🚇 Gare de Lyon

WEB BAR

Funky little cyber café combining art, videos and music daily until 2ᴀᴍ. Good weekend brunches.

🚇 J5 ✉ 32 rue de Picardie 75003 ☎ 01 42 72 66 55 🕐 Daily 🚇 République

SPECIAL CINEMAS

LA CINÉMATHÈQUE FRANÇAISE

Cinema classics with foreign films always in original language.

🚇 D5 ✉ 7 Avenue Albert de Mun 75016 ☎ 01 47 04 24 24 🚇 Trocadéro

LE DOME IMAX

The world's largest hemispherical screen – all 1,144sq m of it Digital sound system.

🚇 Off map at A2 ✉ 1 Place du Dôme, La Défense 92905 ☎ 01 46 92 45 45 🚇 La Défense

L'ENTREPOT

Stimulating programme of French and foreign films, plus festivals devoted to one director. Bookshop, pleasant café.

🚇 F8 ✉ 7–9 rue Francis de Pressensé 75014 ☎ 08 36 68 05 87 🚇 Pernéty

LA PAGODE

A unique cinema hall housed inside an exotic Japanese pagoda. Adjoining tea-room (➤ 72) and garden.

🚇 F6 ✉ 57 bis rue de Babylone 75007 ☎ 01 45 55 48 48 🚇 Saint-François Xavier

VIDÉOTHÈQUE DE PARIS

Movies or documentaries shot in or connected with Paris, or a changing daily programme of wide-ranging film classics. Cheap day pass covers four different films.

🚇 H5 ✉ Forum des Halles, Porte Sainte-Eustache 75001 ☎ 01 40 26 34 30 🚇 Les Halles

Steam baths

If nocturnal bar-crawling becomes too much, why not sweat it out at a steam bath? The hammam at the Mosquée (➤ 52) offers a lovely tiled interior *à la* Marrakesh (🚾 Men: Fri and Sun. Women: Mon, Wed, Thu and Sat). A new though pricier alternative is Les Bains du Marais (✉ 31 rue des Blancs-Manteaux 75004 ☎ 01 44 61 02 02 🚾 Men: Thu and Sat. Women: Mon–Wed).

SPORTING VENUES

Pools and horses

Paris's municipal swimming-pools have complicated opening hours which are almost entirely geared to schoolchildren. Phone beforehand to check for public hours and avoid Wednesdays and Saturdays, both favourites with children off school. Gymnase Clubs are generally open until 9PM but close on Sundays. If horse-racing is your passion, don't miss the sulky-racing at Vincennes with its brilliant flashes of colour-coordinated horses and jockeys. Check *Paris-Turf* for race programmes.

AQUABOULEVARD
Huge family complex with water-shoots, palm-trees, Jacuzzis. Gym, putting-greens, tennis- and squash-courts too – at a price.
⊞ C8 ✉ 4–6 rue Louis Armand 75015 ☎ 01 40 60 10 00 🚇 Porte de Versailles

GYMNASE CLUB
Best-equipped gymnasium in this chain. Call for details on other gyms throughout Paris. Day passes, book of ten passes or annual subscription.
⊞ D3 ✉ 17 rue du Débarcadère 75017 ☎ 01 45 74 14 04 🚇 Porte Maillot

HIPPODROME D'AUTEUIL
Flat-racing and hurdles. Hosts the prestigious Prix du Président de la République hurdle race.
⊞ A6 ✉ Bois de Boulogne 75016 ☎ 01 42 24 47 04 🕐 Closed Jul–Aug 🚇 Porte d'Auteuil

HIPPODROME DE LONGCHAMP
Longchamp is where the hats and champagne come out for the annual Prix de l'Arc de Triomphe. Regular flat-races.
⊞ Off map at A6 ✉ Bois de Boulogne 75016 ☎ 01 42 24 13 29 🕐 Closed Jul–Aug 🚇 Porte d'Auteuil, then shuttle

HIPPODROME DE VINCENNES
Colourful sulky-racing pulls in the crowds. Watch out for the Prix d'Amérique, the top sulky-race of the season.
⊞ Off map at N9 ✉ 2 route de la Ferme, Bois de Vincennes 75012 ☎ 01 49 77 17 17 🕐 Closed Jul–Aug 🚇 Château de Vincennes, then shuttle

PARC DES PRINCES
Huge municipal stadium takes 50,000 spectators for major football and rugby matches.
⊞ A8 ✉ 24 rue du Commandant-Guilbaud 75016 ☎ 01 42 88 02 76 🚇 Porte de Saint-Cloud

PISCINE DES HALLES (SUZANNE BERLIOUX)
Underground 50m pool overlooked by lush tropical garden.
⊞ H5 ✉ 10 Place de la Rotonde 75001 ☎ 01 42 36 98 44 🚇 Les Halles

PISCINE JEAN TARIS
Two 25m pools with view of Panthéon. Electronically cleaned water, so no chlorine.
⊞ H7 ✉ 16 rue Thouin 75005 ☎ 01 43 25 54 03 🚇 Cardinal Lemoine

PISCINE QUARTIER LATIN
A 33m pool with a distinct 1930s air. Solarium, squash-courts, gym and sauna.
⊞ H7 ✉ 19 rue de Pontoise 75005 ☎ 01 43 25 31 99 🚇 Maubert-Mutualité

ROLAND-GARROS
Hard-court home to the French Tennis Open. Tickets are sold months ahead but plenty of racketeers sell seats on the day at the main entrance.
⊞ A7 ✉ 2 Avenue Gordon-Bennett 75016 ☎ 01 47 43 00 47 🚇 Porte d'Auteuil, then walk or catch bus 32, 52 or 123

PARIS
travel facts

AVENUE
DES
CHAMPS ÉLYSÉES

ARRIVING & DEPARTING

Before you go

- Visas are not required for EU nationals, or US or Canadian citizens, but are obligatory for Australians and New Zealanders.
- Anyone entering France must have a valid passport (or official identity card for EU nationals).
- There are no vaccination requirements.

When to go

- Spring rarely starts before mid-May; June is always glorious.
- July and August see the Great Parisian Exodus. Cultural activities move into bottom gear, but accommodation is easier.
- Avoid mid-September to mid-October, the peak trade-fair period, when hotels are full.
- Winter temperatures rarely drop below freezing but rain is usual in January and March.

Arriving by train

- The Eurostar train service from London arrives at Gare du Nord ☎ 08 36 35 35 35.
- Trains arrive at the Gare de l'Est from Germany, Austria and Eastern Europe.
- The Gare de Lyon serves south-east France and Italy, the Gare d'Austerlitz south-west France, Spain and Portugal.
- The central TGV stations are Gare Montparnasse and Gare de Lyon.
- All stations have métro, bus and taxi services.
- For reservations and information on SNCF stations ☎ 01 45 82 50 50 (7AM–9PM daily).

Arriving by air

- Air passengers arrive either at Roissy-Charles de Gaulle airport (23km north of Paris) or at Orly (14km to the south).
- Taxis charge a surcharge at airports and at stations, and also for each item of luggage carried.

Roissy

- Connections to the city centre are: via a direct RER train into Châtelet-Les Halles; the Air France bus which stops at Etoile (Arc de Triomphe) and Porte Maillot; the cheaper Roissybus which terminates at rue Scribe, Opéra.
- The Air France bus and Roissybus run every 15–20 minutes, 5:40AM–11PM.
- Taxis are expensive.
- For passenger information ☎ 01 48 62 22 80.

Orly

- Connections to the centre are via the Air France bus, which goes to Invalides every 12 minutes and stops at Porte d'Orléans; or the more economical Orlybus, which goes to Denfert-Rochereau every 15 minutes.
- Avoid Orlyrail as this involves a shuttle bus.
- For passenger information ☎ 01 49 75 15 15.

Customs regulations

- There are no restrictions on goods brought into France by EU citizens.
- For non-EU nationals the limits are: 200 cigarettes or 100 cigarillos or 50 cigars or 250g of tobacco; 2 litres of wine; 1 litre of spirits; 50g of perfume; 500g of coffee; and 100g of tea.
- Prescribed medicines and up to FF50,000 of currency may be imported.

Departing

- Airport tax for departing passengers is included in the price of your ticket.
- There are numerous duty-free shops at Orly and Roissy airports, but not on Eurostar or other international trains.
- Allow one hour to reach Roissy airport, by any transport means, and 45 minutes for Orly.

ESSENTIAL FACTS

Travel insurance

- Insurance to cover theft, illness and repatriation is strongly advised.

Opening hours

- Banks: Mon–Fri 9–4:30. Closed on public holidays and often the preceding afternoon.
- Post offices: Mon–Fri 8–7; Sat 8–noon. The central post office (✉ 52 rue du Louvre 75001 ☎ 01 40 28 20 00) provides a 24-hour service for post, telegrams and telephone.
- Shops: Mon–Sat 9–7 or 9:30–6:30, with minor variations (smaller shops close for lunch). Arab-owned groceries stay open until 9 or 10PM, including Sun.
- Museums: national museums close on Tuesday, municipal museums on Monday. Individual opening hours vary considerably; always phone to check closure over national holidays.

National holidays

- 1 January, 1 May, 8 May, Ascension (last Thursday in May), Whit Monday (early June), 14 July, 15 August, 1 November, 11 November, 25 December.
- Sunday services for public transport operate; many restaurants, large shops and local groceries disregard national holidays.

Money matters

- The French currency is the franc (FF): FF1 = 100 centimes.

Foreign exchange

- Only banks with *change* signs change foreign currency/ traveller's cheques: a passport is necessary. Bureaux de change are open longer hours but rates can be poorer.
- Airport and station exchange desks are open 6:30AM–11PM.
- For late-night exchange in central Paris use the Exchange Corporation ✉ 63 Avenue des Champs-Elysées 75008 ☎ 01 42 56 11 35 🚇 Franklin-D Roosevelt 🕐 Daily 8–12.

Credit cards

- Credit cards are widely accepted.
- VISA cards (including MasterCard and Diners Club) can be used in cash dispensers. Most machines flash up instructions in the language you choose.
- American Express is less common, so Amex cardholders needing cash should use American Express ✉ 11 rue Scribe 75009 ☎ 01 47 14 50 00 🚇 Opéra.

Etiquette

- Shake hands on introduction and on leaving; once you know people better replace this with a peck on both cheeks.
- Always use *vous* unless the other person breaks into *tu*.
- It is polite to add *Monsieur*, *Madame* or *Mademoiselle* when addressing strangers or salespeople.

- Always say hello and goodbye in shops.
- When calling waiters, use *Monsieur* or *Madame* (NOT *garçon*!).
- More emphasis is put on grooming than in other countries, so avoid looking scruffy.

Women travellers

- Women are safe to travel alone or together in Paris. Any unwanted attention should be dealt with firmly and politely.

Places of worship

- The International Centre for Religious Information (✉ 6 Place du Parvis-Notre-Dame 75004 ☎ 01 46 33 01 01 🚇 Saint-Michel), an English-speaking service, supplies information on services and churches for Catholic, Protestant and Orthodox worshippers.
- Protestant churches: American Church ✉ 65 Quai d'Orsay 75007 ☎ 01 47 05 07 99 🚇 Invalides. St George's English Church ✉ 7 rue Auguste Vacquerie 75016 ☎ 01 47 20 22 51 🚇 Charles de Gaulle-Etoile.
- Jewish: Synagogue ✉ 10 rue Pavée 75004 ☎ 01 42 77 81 51 🚇 Saint-Paul.
- Russian Orthodox: Saint Alexandre de la Néva ✉ 12 rue Daru 75008 ☎ 01 42 27 37 34 🚇 Courcelles.

Student travellers

- An International Student Identity Card reduces cinema charges, entrance to museums, and air and rail travel.
- AJF (Accueil des Jeunes en France) ✉ 119 rue Saint-Martin 75004 ☎ 01 42 77 87 80 🚇 Châtelet 🕐 Mon–Sat 9–6:30. Gives advice on hostel accommodation and discounts on train tickets.
- CIDJ (Centre d'Information et de Documentation Jeunesse) ✉ 101 Quai Branly 75015 ☎ 01 44 49 12 00 🚇 Bir-Hakeim 🕐 Mon–Fri 10–6. Youth information centre for jobs, courses, sports and the like.

Time differences

- France runs on GMT + 1 hour. Clocks change at the autumn and spring solstice.

Toilets

- Cream-coloured public toilet booths, generally well-maintained, are common.
- Every café has a toilet, although standards vary (do not use a café's toilet without ordering at least a drink). WCs in museums and restaurants are often better.

Electricity

- Voltage is 220V and sockets take two round pins.

Tourist Information Office

- Office de Tourisme de Paris ✉ 129 Avenue des Champs-Elysees 75008 ☎ 01 49 52 53 54 🕐 9AM–8PM 🚇 Charles de Gaulle Etoile. Masses of tourist information and polyglot staff.

PUBLIC TRANSPORT

Métro

- Métro lines are identified by their terminus (*direction*) and a number; connections are indicated with orange panels marked *correspondances* on the platform.
- Blue *sortie* signs show the exits.
- The first métros run at 5:30AM, and the last around 12:30AM.

- Keep your ticket until you exit – it has to be re-slotted on the RER and ticket inspectors prowl the métro.
- Avoid rush-hours: 8–9:30AM and 4:30–7PM.

Bus

- Buses should be hailed from bus stops.
- Enter, and punch your ticket into the machine beside the driver or flash your pass.
- Night buses run hourly 1:30AM–5:30PM from Place du Châtelet out to the *portes* and suburbs.

Tickets and passes

- Tickets and passes function for métro, buses and RER.
- Pass prices and the number of tickets required for a journey depend on how many of five travel zones you intend to pass through.
- A *carnet* of ten tickets is considerably cheaper than individual tickets.
- *Formule 1* is a one-day pass, valid on métro, buses and RER.
- A *Paris Visite* card gives unlimited travel for three or five days plus discounts at certain monuments.
- The *carte hebdomadaire* pass (photo required) is valid Mon–Sun.
- Monthly passes (*carte orange*), also needing a photo, are valid for one calendar month.

Maps

- Free métro/bus/RER maps are available at every station and on some buses.
- RATP information (in French) ☎ 01 43 46 14 14 ⏰ 6AM–9PM.
- RATP tourist office ✉ 53 bis Quai des Grands Augustins 75006 ☎ 01 40 46 42 17.

Taxis

- Taxis can be hailed in the street if the roof sign is illuminated, or they can be found at ranks.
- Sunday and night rates (7PM–7AM) rise considerably and extra charges are made at stations, Air France terminals, for luggage and for animals.
- Taxi-drivers expect tips of 10 per cent.
- Radio-taxi firms: Taxis Bleus (☎ 01 49 36 10 10); Alpha (☎ 01 45 85 85 85); G7 (☎ 01 47 39 47 39); Artaxi (☎ 01 42 41 50 50).

MEDIA & COMMUNICATIONS

Telephones

- Most Parisian phone booths use France Telecom phone cards (*télécarte* for 50 or 120 units), available from post offices, *tabacs*, stations or at main métro stations. A few booths still take coins, particularly those in cafés.
- Cheap periods for international calls vary: for Europe, Australia and New Zealand, Mon–Sat 9:30PM–8AM, and all day Sun; for the US and Canada, daily 2AM–noon, with lesser reductions 8PM–2AM.
- Repairs ☎ 13.
- Directory enquiries ☎ 12.
- International directory enquiries ☎ 00 33 12 + country prefix.
- In 1996 French telephone numbers changed to ten digits.
- 00 is now the prefix for international calls.
- All numbers in the Ile-de-France, including Paris, start with 01 unless at extra rates, when they start with 08.
- To call the French provinces, use: 02 North-west, 03 North-east, 04 South-east, 05 South-west.

Post offices

- Stamps can be bought at *tabacs* and mail posted in any yellow postbox.
- All post offices have free access to the Minitel directory service, express courier post (Chronopost), phone boxes and photocopying machines.

Press

- The main dailies are *Le Monde* (out at 2PM), *Libération* and *Le Figaro*.
- Weekly news magazines range from the left-wing *Le Nouvel Observateur*, *L'Express* (centre) and *Le Point* (centre-right) to *Paris Match* and *Canard Enchaîné*. For weekly listings of cultural events, buy a copy of *Pariscope* (with an English section) or *L'Officiel des Spectacles*.
- Central newspaper kiosks and newsagents stock European dailies.
- The NMPP's central bookshop (✉ 93 rue Montmartre 75002) has a comprehensive range of French and foreign press, while the newsagent in the Carrousel beneath the Louvre carries American press and international fashion publications.

Radio and television

- FM stations run the gamut from current affairs on France Inter (87.8 MHz) to unadulterated rap/rock/house music on Radio Nova (101.5 MHz).
- France 2 and France 3, the state TV channels, occasionally have good documentaries and current events programmes. TF1 has lightweight entertainment, and M6 is still evolving. Arte (on Channel 5), a serious Franco-German cultural channel, offers good European coverage.

EMERGENCIES

Precautions

- Watch wallets and handbags as pickpockets are active, particularly in crowded bars, flea markets and cinemas.
- Keep traveller's-cheque numbers separate from the cheques themselves.
- Make a declaration at a local *commissariat* (police station) to claim losses on your insurance.

Lost property

- The police lost-property office is ✉ 36 rue des Morillons 75015 🕐 8:30AM–5PM Ⓜ Convention. No phone enquiries.

Medicines and medical treatment

- Minor ailments can often be treated at pharmacies (identified by a green cross), where staff will also advise on local doctors.
- All public hospitals have a 24-hour emergency service (*urgences*) as well as specialist doctors. Payment is made on the spot, but if you are hospitalised ask to see the *assistante sociale* to arrange payment directly through your insurance.
- House calls are made with SOS Médecins ☎ 01 47 07 77 77, or for dental problems SOS Dentistes ☎ 01 43 37 51 00.
- 24-hour pharmacy: Dhéry ✉ 84 Avenue des Champs-Elysées 75008 ☎ 01 45 62 02 41.
- The Drug-store chain at Opéra and Champs-Elysées offers pharmacies, newsagents, cafés and tobacconists open until 2AM.

Emergency phone numbers

- Crisis-line in English: SOS Help ☎ 01 47 23 80 80 🕐 3–11PM.
- Fire (*sapeurs pompiers*) ☎ 18.

- 24-hour ambulance service (SAMU) ☎ 15.
- Police ☎ 17.
- Anti-poison ☎ 40 37 04 04.

Embassies and consulates

- Australian Embassy ✉ 4 rue Jean Rey 75015 ☎ 01 40 59 33 00.
- British Embassy ✉ 35 rue du Faubourg Saint-Honoré 75008 ☎ 01 42 66 91 42.
- British Consulate ✉ 9 Avenue Hoche 75008 ☎ 01 42 66 38 10.
- Canadian Embassy ✉ 35 Avenue Montaigne 75008 ☎ 01 44 33 29 00.
- Canadian Consulate ✉ 37 Avenue Montaigne 75008 ☎ 01 44 43 29 16.
- New Zealand Embassy ✉ 7ter rue Léonard de Vinci 75016 ☎ 01 45 00 24 11.
- US Embassy ✉ 2 Avenue Gabriel 75008 ☎ 01 43 12 22 22.
- US Consulate ✉ 2 rue Saint-Florentin 75001 ☎ 01 42 96 14 88.

LANGUAGE

1	un	16	seize
2	deux	17	dix-sept
3	trois	18	dix-huit
4	quatre	19	dix-neuf
5	cinq	20	vingt
6	six	21	vingt-et-un
7	sept	30	trente
8	huit	40	quarante
9	neuf	50	cinquante
10	dix	60	soixante
11	onze	70	soixante-dix
12	douze	80	quatre-vingt
13	treize	90	quatre-vingt-dix
14	quatorze	100	cent
15	quinze	1,000	mille

Basic vocabulary

yes/no oui/ non
please s'il vous plaît

thank you merci
excuse me excusez-moi
hello bonjour
good evening bonsoir
goodbye au revoir
how are you? comment allez-vous? ça va?
very well thanks très bien merci
how much? combien?
do you speak English? parlez-vous anglais?
I don't understand je ne comprends pas
where is/are…? où est/sont…?
here/there ici/là
turn left/right tournez à gauche/droite
straight on tout droit
behind/in front derrière/devant
when? quand?
today aujourd'hui
yesterday hier
tomorrow demain
how long? combien de temps?
at what time? à quelle heure?
what time do you open/close? à quelle heure ouvrez/ fermez-vous?
do you have…? avez-vous…?
a single room une chambre simple
a double room une chambre double
an extra bed un lit supplementaire
with/without bathroom avec/sans salle de bains
breakfast le petit déjeuner
lunch le déjeuner
dinner le dîner
how much is this? c'est combien?
it's expensive/cheap c'est cher/ pas cher
do you take credit cards? acceptez- vous des cartes de credit?
I need a doctor/dentist j'ai besoin d'un médecin/dentiste
can you help me? pouvez-vous m'aider?
where is the hospital? où est l'hôpital?
where is the police station? où est le commissariat?

INDEX

CityPack
Paris

Written by Fiona Dunlop
Edited, designed and produced by
[AA] Publishing
Maps © The Automobile Association 1996
Fold-out map © RV Reise- und Verkehrsverlag Munich · Stuttgart
© Cartography: GeoData

Distributed in the United Kingdom by AA Publishing, Norfolk House, Priestley Road, Basingstoke, Hampshire, RG24 9NY.

The contents of this publication are believed correct at the time of printing. Nevertheless, the publishers cannot be held responsible for any errors or omissions or for changes in the details given in this guide or for the consequences of any reliance on the information provided by the same. Assessments of attractions, hotels, restaurants and so forth are based upon the author's own personal experience and, therefore, descriptions given in this guide necessarily contain an element of subjective opinion which may not reflect the publishers' opinion or dictate a reader's own experiences on another occasion.
We have tried to ensure accuracy in this guide, but things do change and we would be grateful if readers would advise us of any inaccuracies they may encounter.

ISBN 0 7495 1651 8

Published by AA Publishing (a trading name of Automobile Association Developments Limited, whose registered office is Norfolk House, Priestley Road, Basingstoke, Hampshire RG24 9NY. Registered number 1878835).

Colour separation by Daylight Colour Art Pte Ltd, Singapore
Printed and bound by Dai Nippon Printing Co (Hong Kong) Ltd.

Acknowledgements

The Automobile Association would like to thank the following photographers, picture libraries and associations for their assistance in the preparation of this book:
Front cover Main picture Robert Harding Picture Library.
F Dunlop 44b, 45; The Louvre 35b; Musée Carnalavet 46a; Musée des Arts Décoratifs 34; Musée Marmottan 24; Rex Features Ltd 9. All remaining pictures are held in the Association's own library (AA Photo Library), with contributions from: M Adleman 87a; P Enticknap front cover inset b, 26b; R Moore 21; D Noble 20; K Paterson 2, 5a, 5b, 6, 25a, 25b, 28a, 28b, 30, 39a, 40, 43a, 52, 53, 56, 60; B Rieger 1, 17, 23a, 32, 44a, 55, 57, 58, 61b; A Souter 7, 13a, 16, 18, 26a, 27, 29, 31a, 31b, 41b, 43b, 48, 49a, 50, 51, 54;
W Voysey front cover inset a,13b, 23b, 33a, 35a, 36a, 36b, 41a, 42, 46b, 47, 49b, 59, 61a, 87b.

The author would like to thank Dominique Benedittini, Christophe Boicos and Andrew Hartley for their help during the preparation of this book.

COPY EDITOR *Susie Whimster*
VERIFIER *Giselle Thain* INDEXER *Marie Lorimer*
SECOND EDITION UPDATED BY *OutHouse Publishing Services*

Titles in the CityPack series
- Amsterdam ● Atlanta ● Bangkok ● Barcelona ● Beijing ● Berlin ● Boston ●
- Brussels & Bruges ● Chicago ● Dublin ● Florence ● Hong Kong ● Istanbul ●
- Lisbon● London ● Los Angeles ● Madrid ● Miami ● Montréal ● Moscow ●
- Munich ● New York ● Paris ● Prague ● Rome ● San Francisco ● Seattle ●
- Shanghai ● Singapore ● Sydney ● Tokyo ● Toronto ● Venice ● Vienna ●
- Washington, D.C. ●

CityPack
Paris

FIONA DUNLOP

Fiona Dunlop lived in Paris until recently. A journalist with a fascination for multi-cultural crossroads and an interest in the worlds of art and design, she wrote extensively on Paris's cultural life for magazines and newspapers. She has also written a number of guidebooks, including the Paris Art Guide, *and AA* Explorer *guides to Paris, Mexico, Singapore & Malaysia, Indonesia, Costa Rica and Vietnam.*

City-centre map continues on inside back cover

AA Publishing

Contents